A Missionary in the Making

By Mabel Tyrrell

Praises for

A Missionary in the Making

In *A Missionary in the Making*, Mabel demonstrates through her transparency that our awesome God possesses the amazing ability to transform ordinary people into "tools of honor" in His hands. Her life is an encouragement for those who dream of being used by God while struggling with inner doubts about their readiness. She shows through personal failures, successes, and uncertainty that God honors simple obedience and can be counted on to bring His plans to fruition.

> *Lowell Stutzman, Pastor of New Hope Bible Church, and*
> *U.S. board member of Mennonite Brethren Missions and*
> *Services in the U.S. and Canada*

Through the years, we as missionaries have visited some of the same churches that backed Mabel Tyrrell's ministry. Being related to Aunt Mabel was always a plus. People expected good things from anyone who came from the same family. We discovered that she MINISTERED to people, publicly and privately. She is still ministering to people, now through this autobiography.

The frankness with which she writes allows this book to be a genuine learning experience. The reader gets to grow up with her as she prepares for and accepts the challenge of missionary work in Africa. If she had written it earlier, it would even have helped me to understand my own daughters better.

There are many valuable lessons for prospective missionaries. If I were still teaching missions in a Bible College, I would want my students exposed to what she writes.

> *David Esau, serving with Operation Mobilization in Spain*

Mabel presents an excellent narrative describing how God prepared and used a willing servant in cross-cultural ministry. Through interesting anecdotes, she presents the intricacies of being used by God to impact others. I enthusiastically encourage students preparing for missionary service and for church ministry to read *A Missionary in the Making*.

Dr. David J.E. Olson, Associate Professor, Prairie Bible College

This book is like listening to our neighbor Mabel talk over a cup of tea in Nigeria as she invites us to share the victories and challenges of her life. How God made a missionary out of this woman committed to Him challenges us to greater devotion and love for Christ.

Ken and Phyllis Lloyd, SIM missionaries

Preface

In writing, *A Missionary in the Making*, it is my heart's desire above all else to honor my loving, patient Maker—the One who is closer and dearer to me than any earthly father, husband, or children could ever be.

I want:

Prayer warriors to witness the victories won in Africa because of their faithful intercession.

My readers to feel the joys, the heartaches, the laughter, the spiritual battles, and the victories that a missionary experiences.

New missionaries going forth to profit from mistakes I made, as both a new and experienced missionary.

I want to challenge Children,
        Teens,
              Young Adults,
                    "Baby Boomers" and
                        Retired Couples
to join the army of missionaries overseas and here in the homeland who are faithfully sharing the Good News in their "Jerusalems," "Judeas," and "Samarias." (Acts:18)

Every real Christian is called to be a missionary—to tell others of the love of Christ Jesus and of their need of Him.

I pray that the following verses will speak to your hearts, as they spoke, and still speak to mine.

"For the love of Christ compels us that if one died for all, then they which live should not henceforth live unto themselves but unto Him who died for them and rose again."
2 Corinthians 5:14-15

A Missionary in the Making

Acknowledgements

If Alan and Cheryl Main had not often encouraged me to "*get going*" on writing up my life experiences, this book would not have been started. Thank you, dear friends.

The writing of *A Missionary in the Making* would not have continued except for the constant nudging from special friends Harriet Chamberlain, her daughter, Anne, Murphy, and granddaughter, Anna, to "*keep going.*" Their confidence in the final result was needed more times than they ever dreamed. Thank you, Harriet, Anne, and Anna.

To the following people who helped edit and proof my script, I am deeply grateful: Karen Olson, Sharon Esau and Doris Notter. Thank you, each one, for the many hours you gave helping me.

Without the valuable time David Bowdoin spent as facilitator, advisor, formatter, etc., this book would not have reached completion. Thank you so much, David.

I am deeply grateful for the following **churches** that have supported me all the way, believing that a missionary continues being a missionary, even when retired from a foreign field: **Ashland First Baptist, Campton Heights First Baptist, Eagle Point Community Bible, Gasquet Community, South Umpqua Community, and Trail Community**.

To each of you **individual supporters** who have stood by me through the years with your faithful support, often at real sacrifice, "*Thank you*" does not begin to express my gratitude. May the Lord show you my heart.

Lastly, to you **dear ones who faithfully pray** for me and whose names I fear to mention lest I omit even one that should be on this list, thank you from the depths of my heart. Your prayers—and the Lord's answering them—have kept and keep me going, day in and day out, year in and year out. You have given this missionary the greatest of all earthly gifts—your prayers.

Much of the material used in this book has been drawn from personal letters and prayer letters I sent home over the years to family and friends. I'm so grateful for their having kept them for me.

Table of Contents

A Missionary in the Making

Chapter 1

Early Childhood

Spoiled?
*I was a missionary in the making
receiving needed, love-prompted discipline.*

As the fourth girl to join the Tyrrell family, my sisters say I was a bit on the spoiled side. That's up for dispute, though I'll admit to the most spankings, the most mischief-making, and the most, if not all, of the trips to the kitchen during dinners because I couldn't stop giggling. But as a tomboy, I think I also had more than my share of fun.

Poor, but Rich and Secure
*I was a missionary in the making
seeing, experiencing things of true value.*

Ours was a happy home, with a mother and father who made us feel valued and loved. Camping trips to Dead Indian Soda Springs and to Bandon on the coast were high on our list of wonderfully-fun-filled family times. Our mother, though not an experienced camper during her childhood, went happily along with Daddy in planning and carrying out all of our family outings.

We were a rich family—in our thinking as children. The six of us lived in a nice two-story home on ten acres, five miles west of Medford. Our dad grew about every kind of vegetable and fruit possible and raised chickens, cows, and pigs. I can still smell the delicious smoked sausages and hams hung in a dark upstairs closet, and see the dried corn, dried pears, apricots, plums, and peaches stored there in bags, and multiplied dozens of quarts of canned fruits and vegetables in our cellar. We ate well. And we were some of the best-dressed girls in our little two-room school. Mother, an accomplished seamstress, made all of our pretty dresses, often from beautiful hand-me-downs from three wealthy, single sisters who lived in the area.

A life-time gift to us children was the contentment both Mother and Daddy exhibited. Little did we realize that we were one of the poorer families in a mostly affluent neighborhood. We were rich in what counted.

Mother was a wife who respected and honored her husband. I can't remember ever hearing our parents disagree in front of us children—not that they didn't have those times in private, but to us, they spoke with one voice— another true gift to us. A couple of us were not above trying to play one parent against another. An example: If we'd already received a "No" from one parent, we would go to the other parent for permission. The question was invariably asked, "Did your mother tell you 'No'?" or "Did your father tell you 'No'?"

Homemaking Lessons & Fun Times Galore

A school teacher before she married our dad, Mother taught us well—taught us many things some folks take for granted. We learned to set a table properly and attractively, to practice good table manners, to show respect to our elders, and to behave properly wherever we were. I suspect that this last lesson took some extra teaching with some of us.

Mother also taught us many lessons in housekeeping, including dusting, which was not my favorite chore. I can't recall her ever raising her voice, even when she found that I'd conveniently missed areas when dusting chair rungs, or piano feet, or the baseboards running up both sides of our stairway. Mother just quietly sent me back to complete my job.

Our oldest sister, Arletta, was away in college at this time. We three younger "triplets"—13 and 15 months apart—had plenty of time to play, even with our daily jobs. I remember the super fun of making mud pies, and of one day finding rotten eggs to add to the pie "mixture." Just once! We never seemed to run out of things to do together. Daddy was a fun parent, making or getting for us all kinds of game equipment. He even made us a standard-size tennis court with a hard-packed granite surface that took months of rolling, wetting down, and more rolling until it had a cement-like surface. Adults, even my Grandpa Tyrrell, sometimes played on it with us girls. Most of the kids living near us were boys, and our place became the community playground. This kept us girls at home, having no end of fun, but always under loving, watchful eyes.

Christmas time was exciting. Getting the large Christmas tree was a family affair. Daddy would hitch the horses to a large sled, and we girls would jump on it to ride up into the hills to get the perfect tree. Daddy would tie it to the sled and we kids would jump back on the sled to be the brakes going down the steep grades. Our beautiful Christmas tree was set up in the middle of our dining room. We decorated it with chains of popcorn and paper, oranges, large sugar cookies with faces and a few silver-rope chains. With a bucket of water nearby, Mother or Daddy would light the little candles on the Christmas tree branches, making the tree all aglow. We could see gifts under the tree—two or three for each of us. Early Christmas morning we ran downstairs to see if Santa had drunk the hot chocolate we always left for him, and to open our presents. I can't remember ever being disappointed with mine, or feeling I should have received more.

As a family, we weren't yet celebrating the real reason for Christmas, Jesus' birth. That would come later.

A Real Live "Toy"

A special blessing came to the Tyrrell family when I was eleven—a baby boy, the only one to carry on the Tyrrell name. And a real live "toy" for us girls. Baby John was the son our mother and father had given up hope of ever having. He was truly God's miracle gift to Mother when she was 44. Little John was the "talk of the town," as friends from all over rejoiced with us over this special blessing. But the poor little tyke was destined to have not just one mother, but five!

Heartbreak—Journey of Faith

I was a missionary in the making
just starting the Christian walk and witnessing
a trust and peace beyond understanding.

Heartbreak came when John was just over a year old. Our precious mother was diagnosed with terminal cancer, with a year or less to live. We children knew Mother had not been well, from shortly after John's birth, but we weren't prepared for the frightening news. We were heartbroken.

The doctor's diagnosis was a wakeup call to our parents, and we started attending a church in which the Gospel was clearly preached. One Sunday morning, not too long after that, Mother and three of us girls walked down the church aisle to publicly confess Jesus Christ as our personal Lord and Savior, and Daddy, to rededicate his life to the Lord he had met in his youth. This began a journey of faith and peace which only a loving, powerful Father God could give to parents of five children, soon to be motherless.

I can still remember the peace mirrored in Mother's face, as day after day, she was forced to trust the future of her baby boy and four girls to the Lord and to a faithful, husband/father.

Following unsuccessful surgery, Mother lay in our dining room-turned bedroom, Bible open before her, feeding upon God's Word. It became her true sustenance. The only complaining I can ever remember her doing was when she would say to Daddy, "Can you stop the girls from fussing?" Just a word from Daddy was sufficient. My sister Margaret often sat beside mother, rubbing her always-hurting feet, and Maxine, gently brushing mother's hair, something she loved to have done. If only I could roll back time and have taken part in those love-prompted acts which brought comfort and a measure of relief to Mother, rather than playing outside.

The days immediately following Mother's home-going are a blur in my memory, but I clearly recall our dad's words, spoken at the side of Mother's open casket. The pastor asked him if he would continue trusting the Lord in the overwhelming task that now faced him, being both father and mother to five children. Daddy's answer was something like, *"I have to. I have no place else to go but to the Lord."* He did continue trusting, with his eyes on the One who would see him through his dark valley. Daddy dwelt deep in God's Word, continually memorizing it, right up to the day the Lord called him home.

A Missionary in the Making

Chapter 2

Teen Years and College Days

Tearing up Our Roots

Shortly after our mother's death, we moved to an 80-acre ranch on West Evans Creek above Rogue River. The creek ran along the front of our property giving us a wonderful place to swim in the summer.

To board the school bus each morning on our way to high school, we had to navigate a swinging, swaying one-person-wide footbridge with sort-of handrails. It was suspended by cables 20-30 feet above a fast-flowing "river" (during some of the winter months). Crossing it was a frightening and challenging experience. Especially when neighbor boys purposely made the bridge <u>really</u> sway—just to hear us scream. And scream we did!

I entered Rogue River High School as a frightened freshman; my sister Maxine, as a junior. Margaret stayed with friends in Medford to finish her senior year in her school. Arletta had finished college and was away teaching. Daddy often worked in the field, with baby John on a blanket under a shade tree nearby.

We were adjusting to new people and new circumstances, but missing mother was still real and deeply painful.

After the initial getting-used-to-everything-new period, I grew to love school, especially sports. Volleyball became almost my first love, and seeing Daddy in the bleachers at all of my games meant everything. I don't believe he missed a single one during my four years of high school. He was father and mother, and also, best friend.

I thoroughly enjoyed drama and publications which were both rather time consuming. I was a good student, but academics were not high on my list of priorities. This became apparent in college, as I will share later. I had wonderful, caring high school classmates and teammates, some who became lifelong friends. Eileen Dick Miller, mentioned in a later chapter, was one of them.

My walk with the Lord Jesus deepened during my high school years, and the desire to become a missionary, given even before I really knew Him, increased. I'd heard and read about missionaries, especially in China, and I admired them greatly. A lively youth group in our Community Church and a pastor who taught the Word fed my hunger to know more of my Savior and to make Him known to others who had yet to hear of Him. That pastor, Joseph Bowdoin, later married my sister Margaret, becoming a beloved brother-in-law.

College Days

I was a missionary in the making
learning that God's plan for my life is perfect—regardless.

The next stepping stone to the mission field was college. When I shared my heart's desire and goal to be a missionary with two favorite high school teachers and my much-appreciated principal, all three tried to dissuade me. One even said that only a fool would follow the path I was choosing. Not knowing the Lord Jesus personally, they could not understand the constraining love of Christ, nor could I persuade them that, *"He died for all and that they which live should not henceforth live unto themselves, but unto Him who died for them and rose again."* (2 Cor. 5:15)

I enrolled in Southern Oregon College, not because it was my first choice, but because I could not afford to go elsewhere. Only at SOC could I earn my way. So why was I against going there? Three sisters, all honor students, had attended or were attending SOC to become teachers, and I knew their academic reputation. Besides, pride made me want to be known as "Mabel," not as "Arletta's sister," or "Margaret's sister," or "Maxine's sister." Sure enough, I'd not been long in Dr. Taylor's class before he asked, "You are Arletta Tyrrell's sister, aren't you?"

The relationship helped get me an "A" in his class. For an entire year. After that I was on my own.

"As for God, His way is perfect...and He makes my way perfect." (Psalm 11:30-32) In retrospect, I saw the perfect leading of the Lord in my going to Ashland to attend Southern Oregon College, even though I'd not wanted to go there. It was in Ashland that the following blessings became mine:

1. Involvement in InterVarsity Christian Fellowship activities greatly increased my desire to become a missionary.
2. The Lord gave me a wonderful home church and family. Ashland First Baptist Church, especially the Women's Missionary Fellowship, supported me faithfully in prayer and helped support me financially during my entire time on the mission field and beyond.
3. In that church and at SOC I met my lifelong friend Emmy Lou Merriman, a faithful encourager and supporter all along the way.

Time Out to Serve My Country

I was a missionary in the making
forming life-long friendships; learning from others;
learning how to live without modern conveniences.

The Second World War was on, and many of our college mates were being called into the service. My high school pal and college roommate, Eileen Dick Miller, and I decided we should spend the summer helping out with the war effort. So off we went to Oakland, California to work in the shipyard. Eileen's teacher-cousin, already working there for a summer, had some pull and was able to get us on as electrician helpers, a step up from the usual entry-level jobs. It even included classes in electrical hookups (lessons that later proved to be valuable on the mission field). We worked in the empty hulls of ships, outfitted with hard hats, coveralls, and all. The work was interesting and challenging; the noise, deafening.

You can imagine the atmosphere in the shipyards. Had it not been for our foreman, a man of character who realized we were babes in the woods, our shipyard experience could have been, probably would have been, tragic. That discerning foreman became our human shield and protector, even making it impossible for us to transfer to a night shift that offered more money.

While in Oakland, we spent many evenings helping in the Say So House, named from Psalm107:2: *"Let the redeemed of the Lord say so."* It was a Christian Servicemen's Center run by Melrose Baptist Church. Mostly, we just showed friendship and listened to lonely servicemen or women who needed to talk.

It was in the Say So House that I met Dorothy Rippon and Emily Steele. The Lord knew I needed understanding friends who would "go with me" to Africa—life-long friends—regardless of distance separating.   Their friendship somehow gave me courage to face new places and new people once I reached Africa.

Many of the service men who came to the Center did not know the Lord Jesus personally, but others, strong in their faith, befriended them and lovingly shared Christ with those whose hearts were open.

Bread, Jam, and Mom Wecks

It was in the Say So House that I met the four Wecks brothers who were stationed together in the Navy. They were from Portland, Oregon, and when they learned of my plans to go to a Bible college, they enthusiastically told me of Multnomah School of the Bible (MSB), located in their home city.

I prayed much for the Lord's leading during my remaining months in the shipyard, and when fall came, I enrolled in MSB. I had the blessing of living in the beautiful home of Mom and Dad Wecks while attending the college.

It was from that precious "Mom" that I learned more helpful secrets of being a gracious hostess. She entertained a lot, and gentle graciousness described her. More than once, when unexpected visitors came, I watched her take out a beautiful silver tea set and fine-china cups and serve tea, with nicely toasted bread and jam. She made visitors feel both welcome and special, even when their coming might have interrupted the day's plans.

What an encouragement the memory of that was, years later, when I had nothing to serve visitors but bread and jam—with tea in plastic cups!

Lessons in a Tent

Shortly after returning to Multnomah for my second year, I received word that Daddy had bought land in a beautifully wooded area just out of Rogue River on West Evans Creek, and that he and John were living in a tent while building a cabin. (After we girls had left the home, Daddy sold the ranch and rented for a time.)

I thought of Daddy having to cook, wash clothes, etc., under very difficult conditions. The least I could do, in my thinking, was to go home and help him and my brother John.

How wrong was my thinking! What a burden I added! First off, Daddy had to find a bed for me and divide the tent with blankets. Then he and John had to quickly build an outhouse. With a third person, they had to haul more water.

Winter came, and to keep us warm at night, Daddy heated stones to go in our beds. (He had set up a wood stove in the tent, so that helped with daytime heat.)

Not even my attempt at camp cooking really made things easier for Dad; yet, not once did he even hint that my coming added burdens. Perhaps he knew of things I needed to learn before going to the mission field.

It was in that small tent that I lighted my first kerosene lamps, scrubbed clothes on a washboard, ironed with flat irons, and bathed in a wash tub.

Many a time on the mission field, I thought back to those camping days and in my heart thanked my patient, understanding dad.

A Death Sentence?

Not too many months passed before we moved into the finished cabin. One day a car drove up our lane and out stepped Frank Hall, the Rogue River School Board Chairman. He'd come looking for a teacher to cover fifth grade during the mornings and high school P.E., health, and girls' deanship in the afternoons.

Mr. Hall had heard that I might be available. I informed him in no uncertain terms that I was not a candidate for the job, that I had no teaching credentials, and that I was not interested in teaching school. He spent considerable time trying to persuade me, even reminding me that my sister Arletta had been a superb, highly respected teacher when she taught in the Rogue River School District. This was definitely the wrong argument to use with me, still feeling overshadowed by my sisters. The discussion ended when I finally agreed to teach if a proper teaching certificate could be obtained for me. I knew it was impossible.

A day or two later Mr. Hall returned. In his hand was a very legal Emergency Teacher's Certificate, with the name Mabel A. Tyrrell on it.

My death sentence—or so it seemed at the time.

Learning from My Students

During my year and a half in the fifth grade classroom, I learned ten times as much—at the expense of my fifth graders—as I ever learned in the teacher-training classes in SOC. And I grew to dearly love those fifth graders, as well as the high school girls as I taught P.E., coached, and worked with them as Dean of Girls.

The following summer I returned to SOC and completed work for my Teaching Certificate, still with no intention of becoming a missionary teacher. My heart was set on orphanage work, with little, motherless children.

Sister's Suitor Leaves His Mark

Before describing the following year when I taught school on the Oregon Coast, I must share the never-to-be-forgotten visit of a young man who was dating my sister Arletta. Arletta and Denny came to the cabin to visit Daddy, John, and me.

While Arletta was teaching in Coos Bay on the Coast, she had become acquainted with Denny, a very personable young man serving in the navy. Denny wanted to court Arletta but wanted Dad's approval. So Arletta and Denny came to the cabin to visit Daddy, John, and me.

Meeting the family was special to Denny—special in that he wanted to make a good impression—to leave a positive mark.

They arrived a bit before supper time and Denny joined some of us in the kitchen and volunteered to help. We put him to stirring a big pot of very spicy, very red-with-tomato chili beans. We chatted together, asking questions back and forth—that which folks usually do when they want to get acquainted.

Suddenly, with no warning, the kettle of chili flew out of Denny's hand and the contents hit the ceiling with a terrific splash. He stared at the ceiling in stunned disbelief while Johnny and I doubled over laughing. Denny had indeed left his mark, and the ice was broken. He won our

wholehearted acceptance and later became another of my
beloved brothers-in-law.

And Daddy had the stove repaired. The burner had, on
a few occasions, shorted, giving one a harmless shock—
without any food mishaps. Denny hadn't been prepared
for it.

Treasured Friendship and Sand Fleas

I had completed my agreed-upon time teaching at
Rogue River, had earned my Teaching Certificate, and had
been asked to teach for a year in Empire, California. Still
needing money to go on to Bible School, I eagerly
accepted the offer and moved to the Coast. It was a good
year, one of learning from a gifted fellow teacher named
Katherine Eskridge. I sensed her heart burden for missions
almost immediately. She became a close friend, a true
mentor. Our mutual burden for missions bonded us
together in a very special way. Katherine became a life-
time prayer partner and supporter. The Eskridge families
continued praying for me and supporting after Katherine's
death—and continue doing so to this day.

Coastal bed bugs! They almost ate me alive during the
night times. At least I blamed them for the little dots of
blood on the bed sheets. I was too embarrassed to speak to
my sweet landlady about them. One day she just casually
mentioned that most folks living on the coast became
immune to the **sand fleas**, so I could take heart.

I never did become one of the "most folks," and one
year of sand fleas was enough.

Missionary Call Confirmed

I was a missionary in the making
seeing first hand that one's walk and talk
can influence another for a lifetime.

The delays in becoming a missionary had not dampened my heart's desire. I needed more training in the Word, and Prairie Bible Institute (PBI) in Alberta, Canada offered a "Search Study Method" that appealed to me. So, to PBI I went and learned how to really study my Bible. I loved my time at Prairie and made friendships I would renew in Africa.

Near the end of the school year I needed to find out where the Lord wanted me to serve as a missionary and under what mission board. I had gathered information from a number of good, evangelical missions, but I needed to see and hear, firsthand, from mission representatives.

They came in large numbers to PBI's annual Missions Conference, many good men and women representing their missions and mission fields. I watched and listened, watched and listened some more.

One particular representative drew my attention day after day—a missionary named Harold Germaine. I was deeply impressed by his love for the students with whom he interacted, and for the nationals to whom he ministered in Africa. And his very countenance, his words, his actions, all focused my attention on Christ Jesus and His love for a lost world.

Mr. Germaine represented the **Sudan Interior Mission** (now called **Serving in Mission)**, a non-denominational, evangelical mission with a Biblical worldview. SIM's "By Faith" and support-pool policies really attracted me.

Shortly after the mission conference, I felt definitely led to apply for missionary service.

Accepted by SIM—IF

I was a missionary in the making
learning to accept God's desires in place of my own.

After I completed a five-week candidate school in Pasadena, California, SIM accepted me as a missionary to work in Nigeria.

Two life-affecting issues—questions—had come up in one of the final interviews. I was ready for the first one, but not for the second.

The first question: *"Do you realize that on most mission fields, there are approximately 30 single ladies to one single man, making it unlikely that most single ladies will find a life partner?"* I had read of the statistics and had battled over the marriage issue, but in the end, I knew that the Lord Jesus would be closer to me than a husband, that He would give me a fulfilled life, and that He would give me spiritual children if He so chose. So I could answer from the heart, *"Yes, I understand. I am ready to trust the Lord in this area."*

The second question, *"Will you teach school? This is the priority need in Nigeria."* I had already expressed my desire to be in orphanage work, so this question came as a surprise. I shared again that I had no desire to teach school.

We talked. We prayed. We talked some more. I agreed to go back to my room and really wait before the Lord for His will. He helped me see the necessity of submitting to those in authority—that it would be essential all along the way on the mission field. The next day I was able to say, again from the heart, *"Yes, I'm willing to teach school."* (It was agreed that I could do orphanage work once there were enough teachers in Nigeria.)

A Voice Change?

As I mentioned earlier, I'd earned my Teaching Certificate by this time (having washed dishes and waited tables to pay my way). Now SIM asked me to return to college and get my degree, which I did that summer.

Among other courses, I took an advanced speech class, not needed for credit, but to change my voice from a child's to an adult's. On more than one occasion when I had been helping in my brother-in-law's print shop, I answered the phone, very professionally, and was told, *"I wish to speak to your father, please."* Or *"I wish to speak to your mother."* It had embarrassed me to no end, and I really believed a special speech class could bring the voice change.

I earned straight "A's" in the class and felt I'd reached a long-sought-after goal—until, at the close of the course the Professor asked me to take part in a college radio play.

I felt honored—until I learned, too late to back out, that it was the part of a five-year-old, and that I would be <u>heard</u>, not seen.

So much for the brilliant voice-change idea!

A Missionary in the Making

Chapter 3

Outfitting Time and Tearful Farewells

Enough to Last Four Years

I was a missionary in the making
learning that it was easier to give than to receive.

1951 was coming to an end and an overwhelming project faced me—listing every single item I would need over the next four years. SIM came to my rescue by sending lists made by other missionaries going to Nigeria. These helped, but just figuring out enough of each item, e.g., toilet tissue, tooth paste, and chili powder to last a full term was mind-boggling.

Friends helped me think, plan, and begin to acquire the needed items. Some searched their attics or storage cupboards for flat irons, kerosene lamps, and cast-iron pots. Daddy donated his cast-iron waffle iron (a real treasure on the mission field). Women's Missionary Fellowship (WMF) groups organized showers, and before too long, every needed item was checked off the list.

Ladies from the community churches of Central Point, Eagle Point and Trail gathered several times with sewing machines to make my dresses. They were fun, laughter-filled times. The ladies made beautiful, modest, cotton dresses, with the maker's name pinned to each one, at my request. Each time I took out a new dress during the four years, I read the maker's name and was reminded of that special friend. The love sewn into those dresses blessed my heart anew.

Daddy had carefully planed and sanded the lumber, and used screws to assemble the boxes in which my outfit was to be packed—boxes that would become my first furniture in Nigeria.

Daddy and friends helped with the huge job of carefully listing each item going into each box, then packing them tightly and carefully for shipping. My outfit then went on its way to New York to the SIM office to await my arrival.

Special Gifts

Among God's richest gifts to this soon-to-be missionary were valley churches and pastors who committed to pray for me and to support me financially.

I truly believed then, and still believe, that the Lord leads most missionaries to make known their financial needs. But for me, it was, *"Trust Me, say nothing to men, unless they ask you directly."* My support was fully promised before the year ended. But far more important was the promised prayer support. I knew I could survive without money, but never, never without prayer.

Commissioned

I was a missionary in the making
learning that others would go with me in prayer.

With outfit on its way, commissioning time came. We chose the Central Point Community Church because of its central location to my supporting churches. The Commissioning Service was so very special.

I had to fight tears during the entire service, especially when I knelt on the platform and eight pastors from supporting churches placed their hands on my head and committed me to the Lord's service. But even more, when the pastors committed **themselves and their churches,** before the Lord, **to go with me in prayer.** I lost in the "fight" during those prayers. At times others in the congregation joined me with tears. The Lord touched all of our hearts when three teen-age girls, ones I dearly loved, sang, *So Send I You*, a song I've asked to have sung at my memorial service—if and when that takes place someday—a message I pray that others will hear and respond to.

So Send I You

So send I you—to labor unrewarded,
To serve unpaid, unloved, unsought, unknown,
To bear rebuke, to suffer scorn and scoffing,
So send I you—to toil for Me alone.

So send I you—to loneliness and longing,
With heart a-hungering for the loved and known,
Forsaking home and kindred, friend and dear one,
So send I you—to know My love alone.

So send I you—to leave your life's ambitions,
To die to dear desire, self-will resign,
To labor long and love where men revile you,
So send I you—to lose your life in Mine.

Tough Love in Action

I was a missionary in the making
witnessing that tough love truly pays;
helping prepare me for working with young people.

I witnessed that kind of love when I spent several days with my Bowdoin family shortly before leaving for Africa. The Lord was beginning the *"The making of a missionary"* in Terell Bowdoin, **my two-year-old nephew.**

Little Terell had somehow wriggled his way behind a piece of furniture and had put his mouth on a live extension-cord prong. Miraculously, it hadn't killed him, but it had burned a hole out of the side of his mouth and cheek.

Joe, Terell's daddy, was a pastor, money was more than tight, skin grafting would cost a fortune, and they had no health insurance.

But they had a Physician God who did miracles of healing. Pastors and other Christian brothers and sisters joined in praying for little Terell's healing. It began and the miracle gradually took place (years later, only a tiny scar was visible when Terell smiled.)

Terell's parents, Joe and Margaret, determined before the Lord to do all in their power to help bring healing—in every way. They agreed not to pity or let sympathy spoil their strong-willed little son. They loved him too much for that. During my final visit with them, I witnessed that love—true, tough love. And it drove me to tears.

Little Terell had refused to open his mouth so his daddy could feed him (the hole in the side of his mouth and cheek made it necessary). His daddy spoke lovingly to his little son saying, *"Open your mouth, Terell."* He refused to open it. The instruction was repeated. And it was repeated again. If memory serves me correctly, after the third refusal, his daddy calmly, gently lifted Terell from his highchair, took him to the bathroom, spanked him, hugged him, talked softly to him, and returned the sobbing little boy to his chair.

Little Terell still refused to obey. The cycle was repeated. He continued refusing to open his little mouth to be fed. For the third time, his daddy gently lifted his little son and headed for the bathroom.

I wanted to jump up from the table and run out the door. In my thinking, they were being too tough on the little lad. Thankfully, I kept silent and remained seated.

Joe and little Terell spent longer in the bathroom that time. I heard the daddy softly explaining the reason for the third spanking. He spoke patiently, kindly, lovingly.

A Missionary in the Making

After a time, Joe returned with the still sobbing little boy, put him gently back in the highchair and quietly repeated, *"Son, open your mouth."* The little boy looked at his daddy—with a look of pure love—opened his mouth and began swallowing the food his daddy fed him.

I had witnessed tough love in action—love that worked!

Heart-wrenching "Good bye"

I was a missionary in the making
learning that following the Lord Jesus costs everything,
even those we love.

Saying "good bye" to my dear dad tore my heart apart. But for the grace of God, I would have turned back!

The parting was made easier by friends from several of the churches who gathered at the train station in Rogue River to see me off. And by a good friend, Joyce Colvin, my roommate at PBI, who climbed aboard and just sat beside me for the first 40 miles. She didn't talk; she was just there with me, letting me cry, letting me feel her caring.

I traveled across the U.S. in a tiny compartment, thanks to understanding Mission leaders who arranged the trip. I'd never traveled before except by car and bus. This was my first train trip, except as a wee baby. Just the idea of properly tipping frightened me. I was prone to motion sickness. I was just plain afraid and feeling more alone than I'd ever felt in my life. But true to His Word, the Lord Jesus made His Presence felt in a very precious and real way, and Peace came—all the way to New York.

In that late November, 1951, I left a beloved family in Oregon to join a large new, unknown one. It didn't take many days in our SIM New York office to know that I'd chosen to be a member of a very caring family of brothers and sisters who were committed to Christ.

The final days spent in Mission Headquarters were rich and blessed, in spite of having to fill out countless forms and get more injections. (I'd already endured a number in Oregon.) The knowledge that I was going to Nigeria fully supported, with a mission family that shared and shared alike, was assuring and heart warming.   It meant togetherness. I was ready to journey forth to my adopted land.

A Missionary in the Making

Prayers Answered

On the High Seas at Last

I was a missionary in the making
sensing, literally feeling the answers
to the prayers going up on my behalf.

On December 13, 1951, I boarded the *MS Roseville*, a spotless Dutch freighter that would be my home for five weeks. Passenger accommodations were very limited, so we passengers enjoyed first-class passage, even eating with the captain and other officers. I felt like royalty.

An experienced senior SIM missionary and I were the only Christians on board, but we were warmly accepted by the other passengers. Sharing our faith with strangers was challenging, just as it had been on the trip from Oregon to New York. Weeks later, I sent the following verses home to faithful prayer partners.

Because You Prayed

Our record begins on a day months ago,
When "farewell" and "God bless you" were spoken.
The train left Rogue River to carry me east,
And precious home ties were thus broken,
But our Lord proved His Word, "Sufficient my grace,"
As many tears just refused to be stayed.
Then down from above came His comforting love,

All because you had faithfully prayed.

Remember the times we oft spoke of my trip?
How I dreaded alone to be sailing?
Again the Lord heard as you claimed His blest Word
That companionship would not be failing.
He sent the new friend, who traveled seas oft,
She's a Christian and knows seamen's ways.
We had blessed fellowship, lessons and tests
As together we spent the long days.
This all came about, I know without doubt,
Because some of you faithfully prayed.

And then let us praise Him for answering again,
As you prayed that I'd seasick not get.
How He faithfully blest, gave health and good rest,
And many fish are all hungering yet.
We can laugh about this, and joke all we please,
But down under I know it's so true,
That most ill I'd have been, yet again and again,
Had much prayer not ascended from you.

Not least in the record of answers to prayer
Was the witness you gave to the crew.
The engineer listened and hungering seemed,
As he heard the sweet Gospel so true.
To others you spoke on the train eastward bound,
To others, the Good News was given.
The Lord blessed the Word as you faithfully prayed,
And at least one new name is in Heaven.

A Missionary in the Making

Chapter 5

New Beginning - Discouragement

My Adopted Land and People

The sights and smells almost bowled me over as we disembarked in the Port at Lagos, Nigeria, and walked down the gang plank into the most populous country (128,771,988) in Africa.

I'd never seen such a multitude of people coming and going in every direction. Then it hit me. These were **my** people, the ones I'd chosen to make my extended family, to live with and minister to for the rest of my life, if possible. An overwhelming love came with this realization, the love of Christ Jesus, for these beautiful black people.

Going through customs was something I had dreaded. I'd heard stories of missionaries' "loads" being opened and left in disarray, and of the need to pay bribes in order to keep all of one's own possessions—something missionaries refused to do. Gratefully, our mission representative met us at the customs gate, and we were finally through the inspection line and out of the building—with our outfits totally intact. Another of God's miracles—**because many folks were praying**.

Unforgettable Experiences

I was a missionary in the making
asking the Lord to keep me from becoming critical of
others. Yes, and to make me thankful for reproof and
correction, needed and otherwise.

Six experiences are vivid in my memory. The first two took place while on board the ship. The next three were in our SIM Guest House dining room in Lagos, and the last was on the train headed to Ilorin.

Our ship, a beautiful cargo vessel, had stopped at several ports along the way. In the excitement of getting to go ashore at one port, I ran down the steps, totally forgetting the "rule" I had been told, that a missionary was to walk, not run, down and up the gang-planks. My senior missionary reminded me again of the "rule". I sincerely apologized for breaking it and determined from then on to be a lady, whatever it took.

Again, I unintentionally broke another rule after we reached tropical waters. This time it was a wise, written one, *"Always wear the sun helmet when out in the tropical sun."* After the second time I unthinkingly dashed out on the deck for just a minute or two to get something, my concerned senior missionary said she might have to report me to the SIM field director. I was hurt and almost devastated. But in fairness, I knew that she had my good at heart and that she was not a well person, the sea voyage having been very hard on her.

It was in the SIM Guest House in Lagos that I experienced three more memorable events, two, not serious—as the third one was.

The first was my introduction to okra—okra <u>boiled</u> with tomatoes to a watery slime. I literally gagged trying to swallow the stuff. It took me back to the days I had watched my dear mother force herself to swallow the just-as-slimy soaked flax-seed "medicine." (I later learned to love fried, crispy okra and onions.)

The next experience was initially heart-stopping. Tiny house lizards raced over the ceiling and up and down the walls of the dining room. During my first meal or two, I clutched the neckline of my dress in fear—until fellow missionaries assured me that the fast-moving little creatures would not drop off the ceiling and down my neck. They were our friends gobbling up malaria-spreading mosquitoes—our dreaded enemies.

The third experience, a devastating one, made me question the Lord's calling me to Africa.

A large group of senior missionaries (senior in experience; not in age, necessarily) gathered around the tables for each dinner hour, and more often than not, negative comments about the national Christians—the very people I had come to serve—seemed to be the main topic of conversation. The more criticisms I heard, the more heartsick and discouraged I became—and to question, *Lord, did I mistake Your directions? Did I miss Your leading in coming to Africa?*

After the third day in Lagos, with a heavy heart I joined another seasoned missionary for the train trip to Ilorin, a city in the middle belt of Nigeria. Shortly after finding our seats and getting our luggage surrounding us for safe keeping, I took out my packet of Navigator memory verses and started reviewing them. The dear accompanying senior missionary (I grew to love and admire her) attempted to prepare me for the heavy work schedule ahead. She warned me that once I reached my station and started a time-consuming teaching schedule, I would find it difficult to keep up with the Scripture memory system I was following.

Wham! Another blow to the confidence that I was in the Lord's will—and another memorable experience making me question ever becoming a "senior" missionary.

I thought much about it as we rode along, watching African scenes flash by.

The train ride stood out in stark contrast to the one across the States because of the soot that continually billowed in and out of the open windows.

Two senior (again, in years of service, not in age) missionaries warmly welcomed us at the train station in Ilorin and took us to the SIM compound.

A wonderful shower and a good night's sleep made me feel like new—almost.

The next day, our District Superintendent, Bill Crouch, drove me to Igbaja, the location of our District Headquarters. My new boss, Principal Dorothy Clark, awaited me there. She was anything but threatening. Not over five feet tall, a gentle lady just ten years my senior. Even though she made me feel welcome, my heart was still heavy, hurting, and questioning the Lord's leading.

A Heavy Heart Unburdened

I poured out my doubts, disillusionments and hurts to Mr. Crouch, a very caring and understanding leader who walked with the Lord and had a deep love and respect for the Nigerian Christians.

For well over an hour, he shared wonderfully true, positive things about the people with whom I had come to live. He told of their courage, of their sacrifice, and of their dedication to the Lord Jesus. He also assured me that SIM was filled with loving, caring senior missionaries (as well as "junior" ones) who loved the Nigerians and were one with them. He also reminded me that sometimes all of us said and did things we regretted.

As doubts melted away, heart peace came, and I was assured that I had come to the place in which the Lord wanted me—and to the people He had chosen to become my new family, both black and white.

Wokowomu – My First "Station"

Almost There

I was a missionary in the making
learning that that my God could deliver one from the fear
of new places, people, and assignments, and from the
paralyzing fear of creeping, crawling creatures. Some of
them deadly.

We were soon on our way to my new home in the school's one vehicle, a bright red pickup truck. Our destination was the Women's Teacher Training College, 45 miles over a washboard road that would take us farther into the "bush."

The WTTC was a girls' boarding school located between two villages four miles apart and was called Wokowomu, meaning, "See Oko and see Omu."

I was both excited and frightened to think that I would soon meet my fellow missionaries and my future students. Would I fit in? Would they like me? Could I be a good teacher, even if my heart was not totally in it?

Dorothy and I arrived at Wokowomu, and Bernice, a glowing redhead from Texas, and Goldie, a lovely Nova Scotian lass, put my fears to rest—as far as their accepting me. I still wasn't sure about the girls, ranging in age from 15 to 20, from many different tribes in Nigeria.

We had just finished eating dinner (supper) when I heard beautiful singing in the distance. Then I saw forty-two dark figures, silhouetted in the lights of dozens of tiny lanterns, wending their way up the trail from the dormitories to our dining room. The students had come to salute (greet) me. Forty-two voices said in unison, "Welcome, Ma," then sang, as only our Nigerian girls can, the following:

> *When my cup runneth over with joy,*
> *When my cup runneth over with joy,*
> *I find it easy to pray and to sing every day*
> *When my cup runneth over with joy.*
>
> *When my cup is all empty and dry,*
> *When my cup is all empty and dry,*
> *I find it easy to pout, and to cry and to doubt,*
> *When my cup is all empty and dry.*

Dorothy introduced me and I said a few words, fighting back tears the whole time. Now I felt accepted by both my fellow missionaries and the girls who would soon be my students. I already loved my WTTC family!

The missionary teachers lived in bungalows containing a bedroom, parlor, office, and bathroom, all adequate but quite small. The communal kitchen, dining and living room were in a separate building. Bernice's tiny office was to be my temporary home—until Goldie went on furlough and I moved into her house.

Facing my "Waterloo"

My teaching schedule included English, Bible, and Math, the last being anything but my choice of subjects. I'd never flunked it, but I'd not excelled in it either. I was told right off that the school's biggest need was for someone to teach math—British math at that—my waterloo. The missionaries at WTTC had prayed earnestly for a new missionary to be sent to them to teach it. And I had been the one sent.

My only comfort was that the Lord's ways are perfect. Knowing how ill prepared I was to teach this subject, He had allowed them to assign it to me for a reason. And I believed the reason was to show me, right off, that I could do nothing in and of myself.

Many a night I wept before Him with my need for wisdom as I prepared the math lessons. I was teaching the senior class, as well as others, and several seniors knew more of it than I. By God's grace alone I survived, and by His grace alone, the students learned and passed their British-set exams. (Nigeria was still a colony of Great Britain.)

English was one of my favorite subjects, and I should have been prepared for the difference in American and British English. I wasn't. Again, it was mostly senior students who very politely questioned my spelling of words written on the blackboard, e.g. "words ending in "re" Vs "er" (centre, etc.), or words containing "ou" Vs "o" (labour, Saviour, neighbour, etc.). Pronunciation was another issue. Girls in the lower classes had looked utterly puzzled over some of the words I'd spoken in pure American English. (Britain had done a tremendous job in education in Nigeria, having started children out in English, British English, from the first grade.) Even word usage was an issue that faced me. Examples: Gasoline became "petrol," the hood of a car became "bonnet", thermos became "flask," flashlight became "torch," and cans became "tins." My students were good teachers, and I eventually learned to spell and speak British English correctly.

Lizards, Snakes, and Scorpions

Snakes, scorpions, and lizards came close to sending me back to America. They scared me to death, especially the small, deadly vipers that got into our houses. Very shortly after arriving in Nigeria, I wrote an SOS letter to prayer partners at home, begging them to pray I'd be delivered from this terrible fear. They took up the burden and prayed. Fear diminished but did not totally disappear. Probably a good thing.

At night I made certain the mosquito net was tucked in all around my mattress and a flashlight was under my pillow. When I needed to get up in the dark, I always turned on the flashlight, reached out under the net picked up my shoes by the toes, and shook them to be sure no scorpion was inside. Then I crawled out, put on my shoes and with flashlight in hand, made my way to the bathroom. I kept a long-handled steel rake inside my front door in case it was needed. It was, several times.

Strong-willed Missionaries Unite

Imagine putting together, on one isolated station, four very independent, very strong-willed single ladies. All from very different backgrounds. Those four people would share the one kitchen and dining room for all meals, would teach together all day long, and would spend any fun evenings together.

They would have no getting-away time to spend at a mall; no way, even on Sundays spent in Omu Aran, to be apart from one another. They would ride to the village in the one school vehicle, the pickup, four abreast in the one and only seat. They would be seated with the smallest missionary by the door on the left side, then the driver, the shifter would sit third from the left, and hugging the right-hand would be the fourth passenger. (Thankfully, at that time, Nigeria had no law against such.)

The above described the four of us: Dorothy, Bernice, Goldie, and Mabel. Our strong wills had brought us to Africa, our teaching credentials to WTTC, and the Lord Jesus alone, to oneness in Himself.

There was no other answer to our getting along happily and peacefully, day in and day out, week in and week out, month in and month out. **The miracle was ours because faithful ones at home prayed.**

Love in Action in the Dark of Night

Long days of teaching often left the four of us weary and needing to let down at the dinner table. On one particular evening as we were eating, I was a bit out of sorts and said something quite sharply to Dorothy who had done nothing to merit it. Immediately, I felt convicted and knew I should apologize, but pride kept me from doing so. Conversation went on, dinner was finished, and we went to our various houses—through blowing rain. My heart was heavy with conviction, but I ignored the "still small voice" of the Holy Spirit, went to bed, and lay sleepless. Totally miserable.

About 11:00 p.m., I heard a knock on my door. Dorothy, drenched with rain, slipped in and said something like, *"Mabel, I know you didn't mean to speak sharply, and I know it is bothering you. Please forget it and go to sleep."*

That dear principal and friend cared enough to come to me—when I should have gone to her and apologized.

It was the love of Christ in action—in the dark of night, during a torrential rain storm.

Fun, Laughter and Old Maids

I was a missionary in the making
learning that laughter is a special gift from the Lord to missionaries.

All was not hard work on our station—usually called "compound." We often had picnics a few miles away, always on broad rock "plateaus." Poisonous snakes could be seen and avoided there, but not in grassy spots. We were continually on the alert for deadly creatures.

On some Friday or Saturday evenings, we played games and ate popcorn in the dining room. I recall one evening that Vic and Louise Carlson from the Omu Aran compound spent with us.

Nurse Louise was a dear, tenderhearted young woman, and her husband Vic, the station manager, was always a gentleman, ever careful not to offend.

We'd finished our bowls of popcorn and Vic noticed a number of unpopped kernels in the bottom of his bowl. Without thought, he remarked, *"There are sure a lot of old maids here."* We old maids (it was ok for us to call ourselves that) burst out laughing. Poor Vic. He was mortified and the harder he tried to explain himself and apologize, the more we laughed.

So many times, a sense of humor saved the day. It is one of the Lord's most special gifts to missionaries on foreign fields.

Chocolate Spaghetti

The week was Dorothy's, to plan the menus and supervise the meal preparations. On one particular evening, we had finished dinner with chocolate ice cream (made in our kerosene fridge), and Tomasi, our faithful cook, had come in the dining room to get his instructions for the next day's meals.

Dorothy handed him the leftover tomatoes and whatever else could go into a spaghetti dish (we never threw out leftovers) for the next evening's dinner. We would be having guests. Dorothy also handed Tomasi the remaining ice cream to put in the fridge.

Not long before dinner time the next evening, one of us checked to see if everything was ready and tasted the spaghetti casserole, the main dish. Ugh! It tasted like nothing imaginable. Onions, spaghetti powder, spaghetti, hamburger and chocolate ice cream just did not mix!

Having no more meat on hand, and with time running out, there was nothing to do but to try and cover the sweet chocolate taste. Surprisingly, enough curry powder, chili powder, more spaghetti powder, (probably other seasonings I've forgotten), and salt did the trick—almost.

Our guests were missionaries, thankfully, and they seemed to enjoy the meal and chuckled with us over the near fiasco.

She Spoke the Truth in Love

I was a missionary in the making
learning how to love even when I found it humanly
impossible.

Goldie left on furlough at the end of the year and I moved into her house for a short time. With just three of us on staff, we were desperately shorthanded. Knowing this, our district superintendent came to the compound with the news of a possible substitute teacher. A very experienced, highly-gifted lady teacher had been seconded to SIM from another mission. Our mission leader was frank to tell us that she had had some interpersonal-relationship problems in a previous place of ministry. Knowing this, did we feel we wanted her to join our staff? We four had been experiencing deep unity, both in the school and as a staff. This made us quick to say, *"Yes, we need her. We want her."*

Juanita (not her real name) arrived and we welcomed her warmly. She was a rather tall, confident lady who adjusted well and seemed happy to be with us. She was truly a very gifted communicator and teacher and soon had wonderful rapport with the students.

As I witnessed students beginning to turn to Juanita for advice and direction—in place of to Principal Dorothy—I became troubled. I prayed much about it but said nothing to others.

But the "little foxes that spoil the vines" were creeping in—into my heart—bringing jealousy on Dorothy's behalf. This was happening, in spite of my quiet hour with the

Lord each morning—an hour when I wasn't really listening to His voice.

Weeks passed. One day, Dorothy, my boss, mentor and good friend, approached and spoke words that cut my heart in shreds.

I, not Juanita, was the cause of disunity in the staff; even the students were aware of my attitude of resentment against Juanita; my jealousy on Dorothy's behalf was hindering the work of the Holy Spirit in the school.

Dorothy assured me that her leadership and her position were in the Lord's hands, and that He would take care of them.

That dear, true friend spoke the truth in love to me. But she didn't stop there. She asked me to show love to Juanita, reminding me that the Lord Jesus commanded us to love one another as He loved us.

Dorothy then went out on her veranda, picked a rose from the bush in a big clay pot, placed it in my hand, and asked me to take it to Juanita—*as if I loved her*—reminding me that the Lord always enables a willing child of His to do what He commands.

I took the rose to Juanita's house, gritting my teeth all the way. And feeling no love. But thankfully, not many weeks passed before the Lord Jesus changed my stubborn heart. (I had honestly tried, each day, to do something for Juanita that His love would do.)

One evening just as darkness was creeping in, I saw and heard Juanita out in the bush sobbing and weeping as she called over and over for her beloved cat that had been gone for several days. As I witnessed her deep grief and aloneness, my heart broke. I was able to go to Juanita, put my arms around her and tell her, truthfully, that I loved her and ask for her forgiveness. More tears followed. And hugs.

The Holy Spirit began to work again throughout the school.

Orphans

I was a missionary in the making
learning that "orphans" were not my calling.

I would at last see the little orphans so much on my heart! About six months after arriving in Africa, I was able to visit the orphanage located in Oro Agor, an hour-and-a-half distance away, over a washboard road. Canadian Mary Sauer, the young, small-of-stature but big-of-heart missionary, was mother to the many orphans—infants to late teens. I had sensed her deep love for the children and her dedication to them when she visited our compound earlier.

On this visit, I saw that love and dedication in action. And I was overwhelmed and dismayed at what I saw.

It was on one of the last days of my visit that I witnessed that dear young missionary prepare a very tiny body for burial, and with her Nigerian helpers, bury the little one. I learned that this task was not unusual, as too many little orphans were brought in too weak, too late to save.

I was appalled. My eyes were opened. I knew then the reason the Lord had directed in my becoming a teacher. As an orphanage mother, a part of my heart would go into the grave with each tiny one, and I would soon become an emotional basket case—a missionary casualty.

On the long drive back to my compound, I said over and over, *"Thank you, Lord, that I can teach school. Thank you, Lord. Your way for me is perfect. Thank you, loving Heavenly Father."*

I reached my station that evening with a new love for my students, my fellow missionaries, and teaching.

My New "Home"

With Juanita's joining our teaching staff, we needed another house. (They had just started building mine.) I begged, literally begged, to be permitted to set up my abode in a large empty storeroom in the school. It was behind the office, away from the students.

We put up wires and sheets to separate the large room into a bedroom/bathroom and living room. My dad's beautifully-made shipping boxes became tables, dresser, stool, etc.

Finally, after many months of borrowing things, I was able to open my boxes and take out my beautiful household goods. It was like Christmas!

The improvised tables, dresser, etc. soon had attractive covers. They were very special, because each item had a name pinned on it—the name of the friend who had given it to me. (I'd put these on each gift before packing it.)

The gifts included throw rugs, towels, sheets, curtains, and lots more. Just seeing the name of the person, as I used his/her gift, brought such a warm, cared-for feeling.

My bed was a high hospital bed, and under it was my wash-tub-turned-bath tub.

A little distance away was my "facility," a very nice-looking bench with a hinged lid. It covered a seat with a smoothly-cut-out round hole. Under this was a topless, 5-gallon can with a slight covering of disinfectant in the bottom. The back of the bench was open, and behind it in the wall was a trap door. Each morning, the hired man would open the door, pull out the used can, empty it, wash it, and put it back in place in the bench. The system worked beautifully as long as I made certain the trap door was closed and the can was in place.

At that time, most of our missionaries had the same type of facility in their houses. It was actually more convenient than an outhouse.

Utter Darkness Surrounding

I was a missionary in the making
learning that the Lord God who indwells the believer is
greater than he who controls all the powers of darkness.

Our hearts were especially burdened for lonely, elderly men and women in bush villages, many of them still unsaved—without Christ. As often as possible, we missionaries visited them.

On one particular visit, Dorothy and I drew near to a tiny thatched hut and made our presence known. Clad only in a few leaves and a loin cloth, a very old couple, with faces hauntingly hopeless, gave us permission to enter. Down on hands and knees, then with skirts pulled close, we crawled in the three-foot door—into utter darkness. Our eyes soon became accustomed to the physical darkness, but, oh, the spiritual darkness inside that little round hut where the Light of Jesus had yet to enter into the hearts of the very elderly, tottering couple. My heart yearned to just put my arms around them and pull them to Jesus. Dotty, proficient in the Yoruba language, shared the Gospel with them. We left that dark little dwelling praying for the total defeat of the enemy who held that precious elderly couple captive in unbelief.

A Human Sacrifice—Almost

Your heart would have broken, had you seen tiny, six-year-old Asabi with one eye that couldn't shut, one little stub of a hand without fingers, severe burns on her face and head, and only one ear. Gradually, as she suffered indescribable agony, the terribly-burned parts of her tiny body had fallen off.

A Shango priestess, bound by Satan, had grabbed little Asabi and held her in the fire in an attempt to offer her as a human sacrifice to her pagan god. An aunt caught her in the middle of her hideous act, grabbed the child, and took her to our dispensary. Missionaries rushed her on to our SIM Hospital in Egbe. Months of painful healing passed.

When the doctors could safely discharge Asabi into the care of our nurse, she brought the little girl back to the dispensary. Nurse Dorothy Peverly became a real mother to the precious little girl, loving her and nursing her through months, years of great pain—loving her to Jesus. One day, in eternity, I won't be surprised to hear Asabi say, *"It was worth it all, to get to know my Jesus."*

Satan Attacks

Always an active, healthy person prior to my going to Africa, I thought I'd bypass the illnesses that attacked many missionaries. Not so. Malaria came first, amoebic dysentery next, then dengue fever, called "break-bone" fever. Thankfully, I had moved into my new house before dengue laid me low for weeks. It was both painful and frightening. All of my joints felt as if they were breaking.

I'll never forget one particular time when the pain was almost unbearable, and fever, high-pitched. A dark, evil presence had invaded the room and a hand was choking off my breath. There was no way I could ring my bell for help from my nearest neighbor. All I could do was whisper, *"Jesus," "Jesus' blood," "Jesus."* After what seemed like hours, the evil presence left the room and I could breathe without gasping.

Weeks later I received a letter from my beloved friend, Janice Paulson, the pastor's wife in one of my supporting churches in California. She asked what had happened during a certain night when she was suddenly awakened with a strong urgency to pray for me. She heeded the Holy Spirit's voice, got out of bed and prayed earnestly, believingly. In checking days and hours, including the time-zone differences, we found it was that very night and hour that Satan had forcefully attacked and was utterly defeated!

Jesus, the Source of My Joy

"Once it was my working, His it hence shall be; once I tried to use Him, Now He uses me." -A. B. Simpson-

Following that night when Satan so viciously attacked, nurse Louise from the Omu Aran compound spent a lot of time with me. She and the other missionaries surrounded me with care and love.

I confess that at times discouragement, homesickness, heartache, and weariness of both body and mind flooded in. Had the Lord deserted me? No! He tenderly reminded me, repeatedly, that He was answering my heart cry for revival—by allowing the difficulties, the hurts, the hard times. I loved Him for caring enough to prune off the "branches" of self that were standing in the way of fruit bearing.

And always, without exception, He restored my joy and enabled me to offer the sacrifice of praise. I was truly a missionary in the making, experiencing the measureless patience and love of my Master Maker.

Two-way Confusion

Two girls had broken school rules and Bernice had talked to them about the chastening of the Lord when His children disobeyed. She then lovingly told them the reasons she needed to chasten them. Someone requested prayer for the girls in a student body meeting. Tate, a senior—you would have loved her—heard only parts of it. Later her version of the correction was: *"Miss Matthews was chasing Alice around because of her disobedience."*

Our English did confuse them. I was talking to two of the girls about Dorothy's return from Lagos where she had gone for passport renewal. Victoria puzzled me by saying, *"When she comes, Elizabeth and I are going to run over her neck."* I didn't get it. She repeated her words. I still didn't get it, so after the third time, she demonstrated by throwing her arms around my neck in a breathtaking hug. Then I knew she meant, "hug her neck."

A Single Male Missionary Visits—Just Once

It was rare for a single male missionary to visit our station at Wokowomu, but it happened when Bernice, the lovely young redhead from Texas, was alone on the station—except for Nigerian helpers. The rest of us were all away for a couple of days.

On that particular afternoon, the single man needed a place to stay until early the next morning, and, thinking there were several ladies on the station, didn't hesitate to stop and ask if he could stay the night.

Bernice welcomed him, showed him to the "guest" house and quickly drove the two miles to Oke Igbala, the Leprosaria Settlement, to ask Dot Hargitt to go back with her to Wokwomu until the next day.

The three of them had good fellowship and a fine supper. Early the next morning, all three had coffee with cream and sugar. One or two sips were more than enough. The coffee was salty instead of sweet. Bernice called helper Felicia and questioned her. The method of preparation seemed ok, so Bernice concluded Felicia had mistakenly filled the sugar bowl with salt. Both Dot and the young man went on their ways.

The rest of us returned that morning and sat down for breakfast. The porridge was rather tasteless, so the helper was again called and questioned. Her method of preparation sounded fine. One of us asked about the amount of salt she added to the porridge. Her answer— *"Please, Ma, Miss Matthews (Bernice) said the salt was terribly strong so I used only a quarter teaspoon."* A curious gleam slowly entered Thelma's eyes (it was her week to supervise the cook). She excused herself from the table and went to the food storeroom which was usually kept locked. There on the shelf stood the plastic bag that looked exactly like sugar or salt.

All of us prayed, amidst laughter, that the eligible young man would never find out that Bernice had fed him commercial fertilizer. Thankfully, a pharmacist assured us there were no harmful ingredients in it.

Thereafter, the storeroom was kept under lock and key.

Still Single and Satisfied

I had recently returned from the December holiday at Miango Rest Home where I'd had an extra week to recover from extreme weariness and lack of energy, often—according to our doctors—the prolonged effects of Dengue Fever.

The time at Miango had been restful, rejuvenating, and fun. Five single missionary fellows, not teachers, were also there for the month of December, a time somewhat reserved for teachers who could be away from their stations only during the long school break.

It was special for us single gals, having the young men join us in volleyball games and other fun times. They, too, seemed to enjoy the fellowship, and they seemed quite satisfied with their single state. We ladies didn't attempt to make them feel otherwise—or, should I say, *"Didn't succeed in making them feel otherwise?"*

I returned home believing that all of us were happy and fulfilled in our singleness—the Lord's will for each one—until and unless He led otherwise.

A Missionary in the Making

Furlough Time

Furloughs Explained

In SIM, a twelve-month "furlough" (later called "home assignment") came at the end of every fourth year spent on the missionary field. The furlough year covered travel times to the States and back to Nigeria, three months that were supposed to be set aside for rest and recuperation, and eight months filled with visiting supporting churches and individual supporters.

In later years, missionaries were able to choose between 4 years on the field and 12 months on furlough, 3 years on the field and 8 months furlough, or 2 years on the field and 4 months on furlough.

I chose the 4 month furloughs (2 years on the field) during the last half of my time in Nigeria, hoping I'd feel more rested, but to be totally honest, in almost every case, I returned to my second homeland to recuperate. However, I'd not have given up a single time spent with family, churches, and friends. Furloughs held blessings beyond description—blessings that prepared me in heart, mind, and spirit to return to my God-appointed mission field.

Reuniting

What a joy my 1956 furlough was, to see my dad, other family members, and beloved friends. Daddy and John had added a small breakfast nook on the two-bedroom cabin, and had built a neat little storage shed in a lovely spot a short distance from their cabin. I asked if we could turn it into a work/sleeping cottage for me. (I would be having all my meals, baths, etc., in their house.)

In just a matter of days, I was settled in and enjoying my dad's good cooking. I'd planned on relieving him of the job during my furlough. He had planned on cooking for me. We met head-on—almost. When he told me, lovingly, that he had waited months to be able to give me real home cooking, my heart melted. What a Dad! I craved four foods: crispy delicious apples, celery, dad's corn-meal supper dish, and his special fried apples. I enjoyed them repeatedly and really feasted during my days spent at home and in the homes of faithful supporters. And gained too much weight!

What a privilege it was, on almost every Sunday morning and evening, and in Wednesday prayer meetings, to share my missionary experiences and burdens. In many WMF gatherings as well.

I often felt drained, both physically and emotionally, sharing in over thirty churches, but I wouldn't have missed a single one of those times!

My heart and spirit were deeply blessed and encouraged as I witnessed ladies' groups, Sunday School classes, pastors, and churches (in the main morning services) regularly lifting missionaries up before the Lord in believing prayer. Many told me, privately, they prayed for me daily, sometimes even more often, and that they would continue to do so—a gift far more valuable than a trillion dollars!

I was reminded anew that those who "stay by the stuff" (praying) make the difference between success and failure, between victory and defeat on the mission field. And those prayer warriors paid a price—attacks from Satan. I truly believed that his hatred of praying believers and their prayers topped (next to the Lord Jesus Christ) his list of "most powerful, most hated enemies."

Daily I praised the Lord for those soldiers on the front line in the battle for Truth.

Disillusioning People?

I was still a missionary in the making
learning to listen, learning to seek advice.

"Mabel, you shouldn't be telling us your weaknesses and failures. You need to give the positive side of missionary life and tell more of the good things that happen. Those are the things we need to hear to encourage us to support missionaries. Sharing the negative things will discourage us, will disillusion us in missionaries."

Those words were spoken by a deeply concerned Christian sister after I had shared my struggles, failures, fears, answers to prayer, blessings, and victories.

I was stunned. I didn't know how to answer her. I realized, really realized for the first time, that missionaries were on pedestals—at least in some people's thinking— that those going overseas to carry the Good News were expected to be above failure, above the frailties (sins) of human nature.

I don't remember how I answered the sincere Christian sister, but her words got me to thinking—scary thinking and questioning. Was I harming other missionaries, support wise, prayer wise, by sharing so frankly? Should I speak only of victories, happy experiences, answers to prayer? I was deeply troubled and prayed much about it. I asked close friends, even some pastors, to pray with me about the matter and to advise me frankly and honestly. Their advice was, *"Keep on sharing as you are—being transparent. It helps us to know better how to pray for you and our other missionaries."*

Recipe for Keeping Young

Five youth camps offered wonderful times—sometimes fatiguing ones—during furlough.

The almost-five weeks of live-wire juniors and high schoolers (four days of college youth, too) were special beyond words. I loved being with the young people, doing everything from camp nursing to counseling—along with daily speaking—along with feeling not-so-young bones and muscles groan as we swam and played together. They were precious times as the Lord drew us close to one another in real love. I marveled—and praised Him with a full heart.

When the last camp closed, I went home to a bed that had never felt so comfortable.

About three days later, company came. I'd warned friends, *"Come if you like to camp; that will be it because of my wee cabin."* Three came and we had great fun. Others came for day visits. Most were friends I'd come to know and love from different mission fields. They marveled over the many natural beauties of Oregon and understood why I'd bragged about *"living in the most beautiful state in the U.S.A."*

Payback Time From a Childhood Injury

My tomboy days, away back when I was in middle school, had a memory comeback—and an after-the-fact-physical comeback. While in middle school, I'd loved field sports, especially track, the high jump, and the long jump. One day when practicing high jumping, I landed on the steel end of a vaulting pole hidden in the sawdust pit. For a number of days it really hurt to sit down, but I said almost nothing about it, knowing that Mother and Daddy would stop my practicing if they knew of the pain. Besides, I figured I'd eventually get over it. I did, and I continued in sports throughout my schooling, not even aware of the injury.

As the years passed, slowly but surely, sitting became increasingly painful. Two-thirds of the way through my first furlough, sitting for more than five minutes caused unbearable pain. Doctors agreed that I'd have relief only if the severely damaged coccyx was removed. Even then, it wasn't a guaranteed "cure," as only fifty percent of such surgeries were successful.

Family and friends joined me in prayer seeking the Lord's will. The Great Physician gave us the "go-ahead" and an orthopedic specialist removed my coccyx. I was one of the "fifty-percent successful" cases, thanks to our faithful Lord and to praying, believing family and friends.

Should I Go or Stay?

I was a missionary in the making
still needing and learning to draw strength from my Savior
for another heart-wrenching separation.

It was almost time to return to Nigeria, and I began to question leaving my dad and best friend. Would the Lord want me to stay at home and take care of him? He wasn't getting any younger, and John wouldn't be home with him many more years.

One day while in town I was chatting away as Daddy drove slowly down the main street. Suddenly he dozed off and slightly side-swiped a parked car. We drove immediately to the police station to report it—Dad's first and only auto accident. The officer was rough, rude, and demeaning. I was so angry at the injustice that I wanted to shout at him and slap his face. Daddy was a quiet gentleman in his response, putting me to shame.

As we drove home, I pondered over what had happened. Did the Lord allow the accident to open my eyes to something?

And then I knew. Even sitting beside my dear dad and talking to him, I hadn't kept him from going to sleep while driving. I realized then that I couldn't protect him from accidents, even if I stayed home from the mission field.

Daddy had never even considered my not returning. He maintained that I was his representative on the mission field. I was assured that the Lord wanted me back in Nigeria, and that He would take care of my dad in ways I could not.

Peace came, and I was able to say another very tearful "good by" on October 15, 1956, and head back to my adopted land.

A Missionary in the Making

Back in my Second Homeland

I was a missionary in the making
being reminded daily that we "wrestled not against flesh
and blood, but against the principalities and powers of
darkness" as we sowed God's Word.

Six grueling weeks of our seniors' practice teaching were over. None of us was sorry. It had involved carefully checking hundreds of full lesson plans, and approximately 600 miles of traveling to the various elementary schools where our seniors were doing their practice teaching.

It had also included the "repairing" of some of the so-called classrooms before the practice sessions began. Were you to have visited one 150-pupil school, you could have seen floors being hoed up, wet down, tramped down evenly, and then painted with "cow-golium." Amazingly, it became a very hard, shiny-surface "floor." Some chairs, desks, and window sills got in on a bit of the splatters—as I later discovered when I sat down on a chair to observe one of our student teachers. (Thankfully, the horribly pungent smell of the liquid floor "paint' disappeared completely once the surface became dry and hard.)

In another building, walls of ceiling board were put up to divide students into three classes, with about 30 pupils in each. The sheets of plywood were painted black for blackboards.

Missionaries learned early to improvise and actually found it a bit exhilarating to do so.

Wokowomu was an accredited Teacher Training College, so each senior student's teaching was observed and evaluated by a British examiner—a stressful time for both students and teachers, to put it mildly.

But far greater than the stress was the rejoicing over the daily 30-minute Bible lessons our students had been permitted—actually required—to teach to over 350 boys and girls.

We praised God for Nigeria's law (British mandated) requiring the daily teaching of religious knowledge in all schools—the Koran to Muslim children, the Bible to all non-Muslims. How the enemy of souls hated it!

A Hilarious Episode—in Retrospect

Domestic Science (Home Ec.) was a required course in the Teacher Training College. It included Needlework (no sewing machines), Child (infant) Care, Cookery, and Housewifery.

Among other requirements in needlework our students drafted patterns for chemises (slips), knickers (panties), and brassieres (bras), and then made them, sewing each article by hand with tiny backstitching.

In the housewifery course, students were required to learn how to polish all of the metals that would be found in a British lady's kitchen: aluminum, silver, tin, brass, etc.

Final exam time arrived and Senior Felicia (not her real name) was taking her practical exam under the watchful eye and rather stern voice of the British examiner—a lady. (It was against the rules for the teacher of the class to say a word during the practical exams in which all instructions were given orally.) Felicia was told in a loud, clear British voice, with British pronunciation, *"You are first to polish the "bross"* (sounded like "loss"). Felicia just stared at the examiner in total bewilderment. *"You are to polish the "bross"* was repeated. Felicia still gazed mystified at the examiner. When the examiner, with mounting impatience repeated the instructions—for the third time, poor Domestic Science teacher Bernice, broke the rules and said, with her soft Texan accent, "Please, we pronounce the word "brass" with a short "a"—as in "gas." Felicia thinks you are instructing her to polish the "bras," the undergarments the girls made in needlework.

Thankfully, Felicia successfully polished an article of brass and passed the exam.

And we single ladies at WTTC became the subject of laughter in more than one gathering of male and female examiners. Some, who had become real friends, let us in on the it. We chuckled and stuck to our American pronunciations.

Ant-hill Ovens

Could you imagine baking bread in a hollowed-out "oven" in five-foot-or-higher, clay, cement-like ant hill? Domestic Science instructor Bernice was teaching the junior class of girls, ages 17-20, to bake bread in just such "ovens".

Some of them were assigned to bake their bread in covered pots over open fires, others, to use the ant-hill ovens. Short of the improvised ovens, Bernice had sent two of the girls to put their loaves in our regular wood-burning stove. Bernice had told them the fire was already going, but to be sure the oven was hot enough.

Sometime later I entered our smoke-filled kitchen and could just barely see Dorcas and Elizabeth down on their knees in front of the stove. Total confusion covered their faces. Suddenly the reason for their awkward position and the clouds of smoke became clear.

I had to fight hard not to laugh at the scene before me. The girls had very carefully taken the burning wood out of the firebox, put it into the oven, and were blowing hard to get it to burn faster. Never having seen a wood stove, and knowing the other "ovens" required fire directly touching the pots—both above and below—they figured the same had to be true with this one.

The whole episode was hilarious, especially when our good, proper American stove didn't get hot enough to bake bread and the two loaves ended up in the ant-hill oven. They came out beautifully brown and baked. So much for modern appliances!

Chapter 9

Dying –They Live

Baby Freddie—God's "Corn of Wheat"

I was a missionary in the making
witnessing the truth of "dying, they live."

*"I will lift up mine eyes unto the hills. From whence
cometh my help?"* was sung softly and tenderly by our
school girls who loved the tiny boy being laid to rest. *"O
death, where is thy sting? O grave, where is thy
victory?...But thanks be to God which giveth us the victory
through our Lord Jesus Christ.... Because I live, ye shall
live also...he shall rise again....wherefore comfort one
another with these words."* Dr. George Campion read those
promises during the memorial service for little Freddie.

The Lord had given this precious nine-month old baby
to Vic and Louise Carlson, our young married couple at the
main Omu Aran station. Each time we stopped there, baby
Freddie welcomed his Wokowomu "aunties" with a big
smile and a gurgling laugh. We couldn't leave without
taking turns holding him. He loved it and he seemed to be
our little boy as well as Vic's and Louise's. They wanted
to share him. Our students, too, claimed the precious little
lad each time his parents brought him to our compound.

Little Freddie became very ill with a high fever and
was taken to our hospital in Egbe, thirty-five miles away.
Pneumonia, along with malaria, had set in. Doctor
Campion fought hour after hour to save the baby's life, but

the Lord, Whose way is perfect, wanted little Freddie with Him. Vic and Louise, heartbroken but victorious, were able to say, *"Our Heavenly Father knows best, and our little son is now safe with Jesus."*

Dr. Campion, with little ones of his own, was also heartbroken. He and his wife Esther spent the night making and lining a beautiful little casket. Some of us awoke before dawn the next day, and with flashlights in hand, picked flowers for wreaths and for a flower blanket to cover the tiny casket. A cross of colored flowers formed the center of the blanket. Freddie was to be buried under a beautiful tree on the compound near his parents' home.

The service was a tremendous testimony to Christians as well as to unbelievers. Many attended. They witnessed none of the usual wailing, blaming God, and the uncontrolled weeping. Rather, they witnessed a Heavenly Father's comforting love and peace—even in the midst of deep sorrow. Its effect was felt in words spoken by one of the Africans, *"Oh, Ma, how my heart was blessed when I saw little Freddie's mother and father smile through their tears."*

Our students were scheduled to sing and found it almost impossible—until Louise—in spite of her own broken heart, went to the girls and reminded them that Freddie was now safe in the arms of Jesus. Many of us, witnessing this, fought tears—without success.

Just a week before the memorial service, Vic and Louise had gone to a small village to share the Gospel. While Vic and the pastor were gathering people, Louise had stayed by the car with little Freddie. His happy laugh and friendly smiles had drawn women and children from all around, even before the men returned to preach.

On that day, baby Freddie had drawn them to hear the Gospel by his life. Now he was drawing them to Christ through his death. Freddie was God's precious "corn of wheat...bringing forth much fruit."

He, Too, Lives On

His life reflected Jesus. I met Mr. and Mrs. Welch and their three children in Lagos, and I was immediately, deeply impressed by the life of that husband and father. He radiated gentleness, and a love and humility not of man. I saw him for only a short time—but in seeing him, I saw Jesus.

Mr. and Mrs. Welch had sold their farm in New Zealand and had gone to Nigeria to fill a real need in the SIM Lagos guest house. They were to offer hospitality to all visitors and welcome missionaries returning from furlough, helping them get through customs, etc. The Welches were supporting themselves.

With no warning, polio took Mr. Welch to Heaven one week after arrival in Nigeria. It was a heart-wrenching time for the wife and children; but also a time of drawing them into a comforting fellowship with the SIM family.

Mrs. Welch, a deep sweet Christian, stayed on with her children in Lagos, continuing the ministry to which the Lord had called them as a family.

How powerfully we other missionaries were challenged!

More "Corns of Wheat" Die

From the human view point, one would say that tragedy had struck our mission. In just ten years, over a dozen strong young men and women had gone Home to be with Jesus, leaving gaps in God's army in Nigeria. With missionaries, especially men, so desperately needed in Africa, we questioned, *"Why, Lord?"*

Ralph Ganoe died of pneumonia. Polio took Ernie Hodges. Arthur Goosen laid down his life trying to save his son from drowning (they entered Heaven's gates together). Earl Playfaire was called Home suddenly. Walter Kretchmer and George Powers were struck down by vehicles on African roads, and Will Carins, on a Canadian highway during furlough.

All of these young men, some of the finest missionaries any mission could have, left behind small children and young widows to carry on here in their adopted land. And carry on, they did.

Four more brave young soldiers enlisted in that Heavenly army. Dorothea Nickelson died of cerebral malaria, Phyllis Kalbfleisch, Edith Waterman, and Dorothy Peverly, of cancer. At Christmas, Gordon Pullen was bitten by their small puppy and died from rabies—in spite of the best medical efforts to save him.

None of these faithful servants died in vain. Were the full stories known, you would hear about many coming to Christ as a result of each "corn of wheat" that had fallen into the ground and died.

She Comforted Us

I was a missionary in the making
seeing first hand the frightening truth that, when the going
gets tough, even tragic for a child of God, others will see
the joy and peace of Jesus—or self.

She sparkled with the joy of the Lord and His love. Edith Waterman was the young laboratory technician in the leprosy settlement near us. She worked closely with those suffering from that terrible, frightening disease. I doubted there was a single patient in the settlement with whom she had not spoken about the love of Jesus. Dr. Campion said the same was true when she ministered to suffering patients in Egbe Hospital.

With little warning, "growths" had developed in Edith's body, and she was flown to our SIM hospital in Jos.

After major surgery, she returned to Omu Aran with a heart at peace, and with the same overflowing joy of the Lord—in spite of the knowledge that her labors on earth were likely to end within eighteen months.

We drove to Omu to see her one evening; all of us were unsure of what to say and how to comfort. As we met

Edith, it was evident that **she** held the secret of comfort—a sweet acceptance of the will of her beloved Lord, and a peace that passed understanding. And the will to laugh and help others do the same—laughter that came from deep in the heart where the Lord of joy was enthroned.

The evening **was** one of laughter as Edith demonstrated, with real humor, her attempts to give herself daily injections, laughter as we bargained to buy her rugs, pillows, ironing board, lamps, dresses, etc.

We drove back to our station, having seen in a precious new way, the power of our God to lift a willing child above all circumstances and to seat her in the heavenlies with Christ—even while still here on earth.

A Missionary in the Making

Chapter 10

Wokowomu Experiences Continue

A New Christian Challenges Darkness

I was a missionary in the making
seeing the warm first-love for Jesus radiating from
Patience
and longing for a renewal of my own first-love for Him.

If you had stepped carefully over baskets of beans, people's feet, babies, dogs—whatever—you would have come upon a small teenage girl with a Bible in her hand, seated with her tiny congregation in the middle of the market place.

Patience was a new babe in Christ, teaching God's Word to three teen-age girls she had led to the Lord Jesus. Her little flock, totally oblivious of the surrounding confusion, was learning John 3:16. Three others, still in pagan darkness, listened intently. The old mother listened, too. She had given her two converted daughters some difficult times, but the Spirit was working in her heart.

A few weeks earlier, the tiny sixteen-year-old freshman had come asking for help. She wanted to become a real Christian and had asked the Lord Jesus into her life. His joy flooded her heart, so much so that she wanted to tell others about Him.

Holiday for the students started soon after that, and forty-one girls went to their homes. Patience, unable to do so, had stayed on the compound with one of the dorm mothers and had become very burdened for the dozens of pagan "sisters" who walked passed our compound each market day on their way to the Omu Aran market.

With a Wordless Book pinned on her dress and a Bible in hand, Patience had gone out to the roadside to wait for some of them. Two girls trudged up the road with heavy loads on their heads. Using the psychology of an educated European, Patience asked if she could help them set down their loads so they could rest for a while. They agreed and sat down.

After friendly talking, Patience began sharing Jesus' love and the way of salvation with the girls. For the first time in their lives, they heard the gospel, saw themselves as sinners and wanted to be saved. Before too long, three girls could be seen kneeling at the side of the road.

But Patience realized that her job had only begun. Asking the two girls to wait for her, she dashed to my house to say she was on her way to the market "*to finish preaching to my sisters.*" Joy radiated from her face.

In just minutes, Patience was back on the road with her two "new sisters," helping carry their head loads the remaining two miles to the Omu Aran market.

The next day I asked her if the girls had Bibles and how they would be "fed." Her quick response was, "*They can't read, but I'm going in every market day to teach them.*"

True to her word, Dorothy and I found her there on the market day described in the first paragraph, faithfully helping her new sisters hide God's Word in their hearts.

Half-buried Alive

"*Help! A little child is missing,*" shouted the hunter as he dashed into the church in the midst of an evangelistic service. The Holy Spirit was working in real power through the visiting missionary, Harold Germaine, the man whose Christ-like life had so impressed me when I was a student at Prairie Bible College.

The prince of this world, hating the spiritual revival that was going on, was on the warpath.

Heading the hunter's call for help, men jumped up from their benches and dashed out and down the many paths to start searching for the missing child. The service ended, but not prayer.

A bit later we could see lanterns being lighted in every house, a guard at every corner, and men and women searching frantically for the little three-year-old boy. They believed the disappearance of the child was the work of the Devil. Had the little life already been offered somewhere as a human sacrifice? No one knew.

Through the long night hours men searched. Every road and path was blocked and people, other than the searchers, were forbidden to go anywhere, even to their farms. Daylight came. The search continued on through the next long night. Christians were praying without ceasing.

On the third day good news came! The little boy was found! Hunters discovered him out in the forest, buried in mud up to his waist or higher. Native medicine had drugged him so he couldn't cry out for help, but praise God, he was still alive.

No one knew, from the human viewpoint, why his little body wasn't already destroyed or sacrificed by those who wanted either "human medicine" or a human sacrifice for their pagan god.

But the Christians knew. They had a God who heard and answered prayer. A God above all gods.

My Three-Legged Dog

"*Oh, no!*" That's all we could exclaim when we saw bloodied, almost-lifeless Audu, my much-loved little mixed-breed dog in the arms of the teenage girl who had rescued her near an animal trap.

Audu had chewed her way out of it—at the cost of a foot. She was almost dead when the girl found her and carried her all the way home to us—something very astonishing; the Nigerians didn't treat their dogs as pets as we odd white people did.

We took one look at Audu, forgot our lunch, and two of us jumped into the pickup with my pain-racked pet and drove to the dispensary two miles away. Our nurses there said we needed to go on to our hospital in Egbe—the only chance of saving Audu's life. They knew that Dr. Jeanette and Dr. George loved animals and would do their best to keep her alive.

I actually had an appointment with Dr. Warren the following day, to have minor surgery done on both hips (deep penicillin infection had set in, not the fault of the medical team, but caused by the penicillin itself). That gave me a truly acceptable excuse for the trip to the hospital in Egbe—if anyone questioned it.

Dozens upon dozens of Africans sat patiently waiting around and inside the hospital waiting room. With Audu in my arms, wrapped in a blanket, I limped up the ramp into the spic-and-span hospital. Embarrassed but determined, I half smiled at the waiting patients and limped faster—right passed them all and in to one of the doctor's offices where I sat, unseen, and held my "patient" (Dr. Jeanette had sent word for me to do so).

After the last human patient was seen, Dr. George and Dr. Jeanette began surgery on Audu. They cut off more of the bone—enough to bring down skin to make a cute floppy paw—and put on a shiny white cast all the way up to the dog's shoulder.

In the midst of the hour-long surgery—done in an office, not in the OR—surgeon, Dr. Warren, walked in. It had been a long day filled with surgeries. He looked at the goings-on and in a rather amused but gentle voice said, *"Mabel, do you mind if we do your surgery at a later date? They have used up all the remaining sterile instruments on your dog."* He **knew** I didn't mind.

A day later I had my surgery and was soon walking without limping, trying to keep up with my three-legged dog and praising the Lord for those kindhearted, animal-loving doctors.

Huge Rat or Snake?

Was it a snake? (I hated the ugly things! I had a dreadful fear of them.) Late in the night I heard something moving along on the strip of tin that kept white ants from going up into the walls. My first thought—a snake! We'd killed a good number recently, and I'd even killed a deadly viper in my house.

I had a box of matches under my pillow (flashlight batteries were dead). After lighting about three matches inside my mosquito net and not being able to see through the net, I decided it was safest to stay put until the "thing" moved to a different location.

The wait wasn't long. Gradually it moved nearer and up onto the windowsill just a foot from my head. There in the bright moonlight sat a huge rat. I froze! (Bush rats are three-times or more the size of American rats.)

I clapped my hands hoping the thing would jump out the window. It didn't. I sneaked out of bed, lighted a lantern, got the rake and started chasing. Suddenly the rat leaped up and out the window and I crawled back under the mosquito net and into bed, hoping for the rest of a quiet night.

It was not to be. The huge rat, accompanied by a friend, returned through the window and both of them spent the remaining hours running around chewing on things.

When dawn came, they silently stole away. And one wilted missionary climbed out from under the mosquito net, just thankful "it" had been rats, not snakes.

Upside-down Lemon Meringue Pie

Goldie gave the cook one of our special-from-home lemon pie mixes to make for our supper desert. He'd made one before—several months earlier--so we expected a real treat

Our mouths were watering by the time we finished the main course and the special pie arrived at the table. Upon seeing it, then upon closer inspection, I'm quite sure we were able to use that special gift from the Lord: laughter.

An almost-raw crust covered what looked somewhat like meringue, which in turn covered a very runny-looking lemon-pie filling.

Thankfully, we had fresh fruit on hand and enjoyed it for our desert.

No Time to Lose—a Baby is Coming!

I was a missionary in the making
learning that one needs to be ready for any experience.

An African pastor rushed up to us saying, *"Please, a woman is about to deliver and she can't make it to the dispensary. Will you help carry her there?"*

Of course there was no answer but, *"Yes."* (The pastor had already brought the young mother, even then in labor, on the back of his motorcycle to the first village 2 miles away.)

We rushed to the kitchen, grabbed a teakettle of boiling water, a dish pan in which to "catch baby," two small hand towels, a ball of general-purpose twine, and the all-purpose scissors.

Dorothy had seen a few babies delivered years before. I'd seen none. So the pastor and Dorothy were to ride in the back of the pickup with the soon-to-be mother.

Two miles out, we picked up the lady. Dorothy sat on a bench in the back, with her arms around the woman kneeling in front of her. Pastor held the tea kettle of hot water. I, one scared "ambulance" driver, started rather slowly over the pot-holed, washboard road. However, one backward glance told me to step on the gas. The expectant mother, well along in labor, had her arms around Dorothy's neck almost strangling her. I stepped harder on the gas. The poor pastor gripped the tea kettle with hot water leaping out the spout each time we dropped into a pothole.

We made it to the dispensary, jumped out, and looked for the midwife to take over. No midwife!

As a couple of men lifted the woman onto a canvas stretcher, we saw that her water had broken and the baby was already on its way into the world—with the cord tight around its neck. Still no midwife and the baby was turning blue. We loosened the cord and the little one began to breathe.

Then the midwife arrived. She finished delivering a tiny baby girl. The mother, unaided, climbed down from the table and walked into the next room. Dorothy and I collapsed on a bench nearby.

Heartbreaking News from the Homeland

I was a missionary in the making
needing to draw deeply from the God of all comfort.

About halfway through my second term on the field, I needed rather major surgery due to a large ovarian tumor (non-malignant). I had the surgery in our SIM Hospital in Jos (our missionary doctors and nurses were wonderfully skilled and caring). Recovery came rapidly, and after several weeks of recuperating, I returned to my station.

I'd been back just a few days when a bicycle messenger rode into the compound with a telegram. Always, when one of those frightening yellow envelopes arrived for a missionary, another would receive it and would be with the one to whom it was addressed —to try and soften any shocking news. Not so in this case. I was outside when the boy arrived and I took the telegram. My name was on it—a telegram from my sister Margaret saying our beloved dad had gone to be with the Lord. No details were given. Not a single one. I was stunned, shocked, devastated. Imagination ran wild. I began to think that news of my surgery had caused my dad's death through a heart attack (I'd written him about it).

Weeks passed and no letters came telling me what took our dad, weeks of not understanding why no word came from Margaret or other family members. God's "perfect" will? My heart and head disagreed—in this case—and I grieved far longer than I should have.

The time came when we needed food supplies from Ilorin, the location of our SIM Business Department. Several of us made the 50-mile trip. Weeks before, we had ordered boxes of canned milk that were in the BD waiting to be picked up.

We made our purchases, journeyed back to our station and proceeded to open up boxes of food stuff. As the lid came off one wooden box, we saw a layer of letters on top of the cans of milk. They were addressed to Mabel Tyrrell. The letters had arrived weeks before, and truly caring fellow missionaries, thinking we were coming in immediately for the supplies, had put my letters in the box for safe delivery.

Those letters gave the longed-for information. Margaret and others had written immediately after Daddy's death, telling me he had gone peacefully to sleep one night and awakened in Heaven—no known cause of death. Daddy had been in Shady Cove the evening before, played baseball with the Bowdoin children, returned home, went to bed that night, and awakened in Heaven.

I was heart-stricken all over again, but I did turn more fully to my Heavenly Father for comfort.

From the time of our dad's death and on, my beloved sister Margaret took his place in writing to me every single week of every month, of every year.

Second Furlough

Closure at Last

Heartache kept me from wanting to go home on the furlough that was due several months after Daddy's death, but health required it. It wouldn't be home without my dad. Brother John had married and he and my precious sister-in-law Charlene and their children were living in Dad's place. I moved into my special little cottage behind their house and tried to adjust.

I understood for the first time what people meant when they spoke of "closure" after losing a loved one. I'd not had it after Daddy's passing, and my only solace seemed to be in visiting the cemetery where he was buried. Almost no one understood, and I couldn't explain. Family reminded me that our dear dad was not there, just his shell. I knew this in my head, but my heart refused to accept it. Never again would I question another who seems to grieve "too long."

I'd not turned from the Lord Jesus; I just hadn't let go and allowed Him to heal the deep hurt in my heart.

He was so gentle and patient, and as never before, I was experiencing His tender mercies that were new every single morning—and all day long—and through the deep hours of night time when memories crept in with tears and sleep refused to come. People were praying earnestly for me, and closure finally came.

Visiting individual supporters and supporting churches helped me get back on track emotionally—and spiritually. I could finally truly understand and apply the words of 2 Corinthians 1:3-4

"Praise be to the God of all comfort...who comforts us in all our trouble, so that we can comfort those in any trouble with the comfort wherewith we ourselves are comforted from God."

It was soon after that furlough that our dad's place was sold and my Bowdoin family made it very clear that their home was to become my home each following furlough, if I so chose. What a comfort that was to me!

Chapter 12
Dec 1961-June1966

Egbe—My Second "Station"

New Home and Family

I was a missionary in the making
needing more than ever to find my sufficiency in the Lord
Jesus as I faced a classroom of boys.

In 1962, I returned to Nigeria and settled into my new home on the campus (compound) of Titcombe College, located in the village of Egbe, the same village in which one of our SIM Hospitals was located (the one to which I had taken my dog, Audu).

My new abode was a nice one-bedroom cottage with all I needed for independent living, having a complete kitchen setup. Being on my own was a delightful experience. I cooked what I wanted, ate when I wanted, and spent evenings alone—when I wanted to. The three other single missionary ladies (all of them friendly, lovable people) shared a common dining room and ate all of their meals together. They, and even some of the married folks, said I'd be too lonely. I told them to ask me after a few weeks—or a month—if being so independent was a blessing or otherwise. I had a suspicion my answer would be, "Both." And it was.

I thoroughly enjoyed being completely on my own for a time, but eventually I missed the meal-time fellowship.

My good friend, Dorothy, had also been transferred to Egbe, and after several months, we began eating together.

The mission family at Wokowomu changed somewhat over the eight years I was there, but we had never been more than eight people, including one married couple, living on the station. Egbe was a different story with its large population of missionaries. One single guy, four single ladies, and a fair number of married couples were on the Titcombe College Staff—in addition to a number of Nigerian teachers. The SIM Hospital and Nurses Training School (across the road) had a fairly large staff of both married couples and single ladies.

My new family, though large, was a close-knit, caring one, united in the love of Jesus. Fellowship was deep and sweet. Principal Charlie Frame and his wife Betty went out of their way to make the single missionaries feel needed and wanted. It was a good feeling.

Uncrossable Rivers and Mountains

I needed that feeling when I began working there at Titcombe College, a boys' secondary school and junior college. Just the thought of standing before large classes of boys—almost young men—really frightened me. I didn't think I could do it, but I actually had no choice in the matter. I had sealed my fate many years back when I agreed to do whatever the mission leaders felt I should do, believing then, and still believing, that they knew best. One of my former high school students, now a college graduate teaching in a secondary school, hadn't added to my peace of mind when she said, *"Miss Tyrrell, remember that they (the male students) will try you, just as they do every new teacher, especially women."* How truly she "prophesied."

Titcombe College had high academic ratings with other accredited schools in Nigeria. Most of the high school seniors and junior college graduates earned high marks on the British-moderated West African School Certificate examinations, thanks to a very committed faculty of SIM missionary teachers. Even more importantly, thanks to a faithful Lord God who gave to each teacher the needed wisdom and energy to do a job honoring to His name. **And to prayer warriors in the homelands who faithfully upheld them in prayer.**

I joined that group of dedicated teachers (most had second degrees; a few, third) feeling unqualified to fill the positions to which I was assigned: librarian and English teacher. Josie, a very gifted, young English lass, had gone on furlough, and I was to take her place. I was told she could easily do three people's work and still keep sweet, efficient, and off sleeping pills. Her shoes I could not fill.

There were actually three library sections with over 6,000 non-fiction books, as well as much fiction. One of my responsibilities, with good student library aides, was to change the whole library setup to the Dewey Decimal System (I almost memorized Mr. Dewey's Classification Manual). Some days, as I looked at the books yet to be classified—and all that went with changing the whole library system—I almost panicked. At those times the Lord reminded me of the promise in a chorus the missionaries often sang:

"Got any rivers you think are uncrossable. "Got any mountains you can't tunnel through? God specializes in things thought impossible. And He can do what no other one can do."

I knew right from "get-go" that only the Lord Jesus could get me over the deep rivers ahead, and through the high mountains—in both the library and in the classrooms full of boys.

And He did just that—because of the faithful prayers of dear ones in the homelands.

A Missionary's Plea

During the early struggles there at Titcombe College, I sent home to family and friends the following missionary's plea:

Do you hear (us) pleading, pleading,
Not for wealth, comfort, power
But that you, a Christian brother
Will but set aside an hour,
Wherein (we'll) be remembered
Daily at the Throne of Grace
That the work which (we) are doing
In your life may have a place?

Do you know that (we) are longing
For the sympathetic touch
That is (ours) when friends are praying
In the homeland very much.
That our God will bless the efforts
(We) are making in His name,
And for souls for whom (we're) working,
With His love may be aflame?

Do you see (us), seeking, seeking
For the gift of priceless worth
That (we) count of more importance
Than all other gifts of earth?
Not the gold from rich man's coffers,
Nor relief from any care—
'Tis the gift that you can give (us)—
'Tis the Christian's daily prayer.
-Selected-

Itching and Coughing

I was a missionary in the making
experiencing again, first hand, the compassionate ministry
of our missionary doctors and nurses.

I was back at Egbe, about two years into my time at Titcome College, when I started having severe itching and coughing which almost drove me up the wall—and sometimes to tears. It went on for weeks before the cause was found. Dr. George tirelessly tested, retested, searched and researched. (I knew he and others prayed.) At last the culprit was found. Filariasis. It was a tropical disease caused by parasitic worms or their larvae, transmitted by insect bites. Dr. George began a series of injections and gradually, over a period of weeks, the terrible itching and coughing stopped. When the filariasis was gone, I felt like a new person. A deeply grateful one. I praised God for Dr. George Campion and our lab technicians. And for fellow missionaries who showed me nothing but love when they could so easily and understandably have avoided me and the constant coughing that accompanied the itching.

People in our homelands had no idea how blessed we in SIM were with medical specialists in almost every field, and well-trained, dedicated nurses and technicians. Our doctors took very seriously the health of missionaries, often working round the clock to keep us on our feet—or to get us back up on them. And they did it with endless patience and caring. They showed equal concern and compassion for the Nigerian patients. Often, their only pay was a heartfelt "Thank you."

I doubt that many folks know that in SIM, doctors, lawyers, folks with three degrees or more to their names, all received the same missionary allowance as every other missionary. What financial sacrifices many of the professional men and women made when they joined SIM with its share-and-share-alike policy!

Cutting God's "Curtains"

I was a missionary in the making
learning to really listen each morning to the Lord's
instructions—lest...

Little black eyes loved peeking in the missionaries' windows to watch the strange white people. To prevent this, my Nigerian helper drew the lovely flowered curtains—covered with large red and yellow roses surrounded by green leaves—over my front windows each afternoon before she left for home.

Something had gouged a two-inch-deep place on the side of one of the curtains. It was a foot above the window sill. Before going to school one morning, I showed Abigail the damaged area and explained that I wanted her to cut off the side of the curtain, bottom to top, and then hem the raw edge. I explained in English and wanted to do so in Yoruba, but Abigail insisted she understood. I went off to school and forgot about curtains.

I was horrified when I walked up my driveway that evening and looked at the front of my house. True to my instructions, Abigail had drawn the curtains across the windows, curtains that were <u>all</u> a foot above the window sills. Little children would have had a ball peeking in all three windows.

Laugh? Cry? Get angry? I could have done all three when I saw what she had done. It was a good thing Abigail had gone home before I arrived because I did all three—in reverse order.

Always seeking to please me, my loyal helper must have worked very hard all day long hemming up the six curtains, using beautiful, small stitches. I doubt she had even stopped to eat lunch.

If only she had really **listened** to my words, my instructions given early that morning!

Before leaving for school the next day, I was able to calmly show her the mistake and ask her to carefully join the cut-off bottoms of the curtains to their tops. This required tiny back-stitching; even more time-consuming than tiny hemming stitches (I had no sewing machine).

I returned that evening to find that no little eyes could peek in my windows. Pieces of red roses often joined parts of yellow roses, with green leaves in odd places on the curtains. I knew that Abigail had again worked her heart out to please me.

And what a lesson I learned! I purposely kept those mismatched curtains on my windows for a number of years to remind me each morning to really hear and understand the Lord's instructions—lest I "miscut" His "curtains."

A Spitting Cobra Across Our Path

It was a dark, cloudy night. The faint light from the tiny lantern shone through the shadows just a few feet ahead of us. Christiana, a dear Nigerian sister, and I made our way slowly up the road to my house. Dorothy, a short distance behind, was doing her usual thing, looking for stars—in spite of the clouds. She and Christy were a pair; one often went without a light; the other one studied the heavens. And I kept eyes glued to the ground watching for snakes.

We had reached my yard when suddenly our dim light spotted a long, black ribbon—a huge one. I screamed, "*Snake!*" We stopped in our tracks and began yelling for help.

The cobra was far too big for us ladies to kill. Two of us kept shouting and trailing along at a safe distance (it was an unwritten law that one did not allow a dangerous snake to get out of sight) while Christy ran to the house for a brighter light. Justice, a Nigerian brother heard our cry, came running, took one look at the huge reptile and dashed to his house for a gun. Returning with it, he exclaimed, "*The snake is so big I can't kill it unless I can hit its head.*"

The spitting cobra was moving faster and our lights were wavering. "*Hold the lights steady,*" Justice shouted.

Suddenly we heard a loud explosion and saw the huge snake begin to writhe and wriggle off into a pit. Another shot, a direct hit on its head, and the cobra was mortally wounded.

A short time later a crowd of boys gathered around, fished the dead snake out of the pit and took it home. We knew they would skin it, cut large white snake steaks, call friends, and have a wonderful feast.

We three moved shakily on to my house, thanking the Lord. Many people in Nigeria had been fatally bitten by snakes. It could so easily have happened to us.

Chapter 13

Mopa Experiences – My Third "Station"

Another Close-knit Family

I was a missionary in the making
facing new, rather daunting challenges.

In June of 1966, I moved to our SIM compound in the village of Mopa and joined a very small mission family. Mary, Sarah, and Mitch made me feel one of them right off, and they helped give me courage to face some real challenges that lay ahead.

The first challenge was my "new" home—a very old house that hadn't been occupied—by people—for several years. My "roommates" had lived there for many years and they weren't about to move out.

One evening, early in my time there, I sat at my desk doing lesson plans in the soft glow of a kerosene lamp. Suddenly a huge rat lunged out of nowhere and headed right for me. I screamed and jumped to higher ground—the seat of a chair. Mary, living next door, heard my scream, came to the rescue and said, "Mabel, it's **just** a rat."

After two weeks of seeing six rat-trap victims (dead ones) from six different nights, and no letup of roving rodents in my house, I'd had enough.

A Nigerian worker and I chipped and ripped up a twelve-year-old linoleum that covered a network of hundreds of dead yet still-clinging grass roots—and more. Then a mason and I filled all the valleys and ditches in the cement floor and painted it. My helper next tackled holes in the walls and large cracks around doors. In the end I no longer needed to jump on chairs to escape unwelcome visitors. I almost loved that old house—once I was the only occupant.

Mopa Secondary School, under the sponsorship of ECWA, our Nigerian arm of SIM, had recently opened. The principal needed a missionary teacher to assist for six months with the teaching of English and to set up a library, and I was asked to fill the need. It was both exciting and a bit frightening, for the first time being the only white person in a school, working under a Nigerian principal.

The second challenge was the obstacle course on the way to school. I rode a motor bike to the school located about two miles from our compound. It was a driver's nightmare of road obstacles that included dogs, sheep, goats, pigs, chickens, and dozens of children headed to the public elementary school in the direction from which I had come. More than once as I swerved to miss dogs racing almost at me, I was met with people's glares and sometimes words I couldn't understand, thankfully. I tried to smile and wave to folks on each trip to and from school, but that in itself was dangerous, especially taking one hand off the handlebars when zigging and zagging between obstacles.

I doubt I ever reached the school—or home at end of day—without saying, *"Thank you, Lord, thank you, Lord, for your protection."*

The French-type "facility" was the third challenge. It was a very tiny walled-only room. A large round hole in the cement floor was the only "commode." Nigerian girls had no trouble with it. Not so, the missionary. The solution: a specially-built three-sided box with a round hole in the top. When needed, the box was moved over the hole in the floor. It was for *"our white Mother only."* The students were warned not to <u>even try</u> using it. Thankfully, the little room had a door with a hook for safe closure. I carried my tissue with me and found this to be a totally satisfactory "facility"—for six months.

Setting up a library was the fourth challenge. In reorganizing the entire library back at Titcombe College, I had been given permission to pull and discard all of the books that were beyond mending. They had been offered to, of all people, William, the Mopa School Principal. And he had delightedly accepted them.

It was mainly with those "beyond repair" books that I went to work setting up the MSS library. The job was a time-and-energy-consuming challenge, and I chuckled often as I mended the un-mendables to help set up the school's "new" library.

The fifth challenge came when issues arose in which, it seemed to me, gray areas of honesty were in play. I mentioned this to one of our mission leaders when asked how things were going. His reply was something like, *"Mabel, you are going to be shocked to see "gray areas" creeping into the American way of life—even among Christians."* I really didn't believe him. Until I was home one furlough. I share that experience in a later chapter.

My first five months teaching in the Mopa Secondary School were hard and easy, wonderful and discouraging—total contradictions. Many of the secondary school boys and girls (a co-education, non-boarding school), were lovable, cooperative, and industrious. Not so, a small core of others who tried me daily, mostly through their "eye talking" with one another. It was a real skill the Nigerians had—communicating by eye. The small group of students did it continually while I was teaching. It brought almost to tears more than once and greatly affected the class atmosphere. There seemed little I could do about it.

I disliked that small group of students. I confessed it to the Lord and asked Him to take over in my heart. He did just that, filling it with His love for those troublesome teens. They didn't change. I did. But in spite of the change, I'd still go home at end of some days emotionally drained and physically fatigued.

At the close of an especially hot and humid one, I reached my house feeling at the end of my rope. I plunked myself down on the edge of the "cool" cement bathtub (first room I entered from the back door), looked through my mail and found some church bulletins from home. On the bottom of one was printed, *"Remember to pray for Mabel in Nigeria."*

I just sat there and wept. The tears and message brought healing and I got up renewed in both spirit and body.

The eye talking didn't stop during the remaining months, but I was able to ignore it—almost—and focus my attention on the rest of the class. I still didn't like those teens, but I loved them. A very real miracle—**because folks in the homeland were definitely *"remembering to pray for Mabel."***

Bugs and Bifocals

I thoroughly enjoyed visiting in Nigerian homes and eating Nigerian food, especially rice and beans with hot pepper gravy.

The women soaked the beans to bring to the top beans that refused to give up little black weevils; such were discarded. The process was repeated two times before the "clean" beans were put on to boil. Tomatoes, onions, and red-hot peppers were all "blended" on grinding stones, added to peanut oil and boiled down to a thick gravy. It was poured over the cooked rice and beans and the dish was delicious.

I loved the combination and enjoyed every bite of it when I ate with friends in the village, usually in fairly dark rooms amidst happy visiting. I decided to make it an almost-daily part of my home-cooked diet.

There was just one problem: When I began preparing it, I noticed that just two soakings didn't get rid of all the weevils. Neither did three, nor four soakings, and less than half of my beans remained to be cooked. I knew that was too wasteful, too expensive.

The solution? I followed their method of preparation— two soakings only—and before sitting down to eat, I removed my bifocals. I actually enjoyed my rice and bean dinners, saved money, and had more protein in my diet. Mind over matter for sure.

Great Food Substitutes

Potato salad, potato chips, apple pie, and strawberry jello— American foods we missionaries sometimes craved. And there were unique ways to satisfy our cravings.

"Nigerian potato salad": We boiled green, rock-hard bananas in the skins, then pealed and cubed them as one would cube boiled potatoes. To those were added lots of chopped onions, cut-up boiled eggs, celery salt, salt, pepper, and good homemade mayonnaise. After the combination had set for several hours to absorb all of the flavors, an amazing "potato" salad resulted. I doubt most folks would have guessed that green bananas were the basic ingredient.

"Potato" chips: Almost-green bananas came to the rescue again. We peeled and sliced them almost paper thin, using potato peelers. Deep fried in peanut oil, the chips were a great substitute for potato chips.

"Apple pie": We peeled and finely sliced very green papayas, generously sprinkled the slices with lemon juice and left them to soak up the lemon flavor before adding salt, sugar and apple-pie spices. Baked in a flakey crust (made with oil), the apple pie became a prize winner.

"Strawberry jello": Most missionaries took different flavors of jello to the field with them, hoarding the jello for special occasions. I especially liked strawberry with "real" strawberries. To make it we put delicious red guavas through a sieve and added the seedless fruit to thickening jello. Whipped "cream" (made from canned milk) topped the jello, making a delicious strawberry dessert.

We were definitely not "poor, diet-restricted" missionaries.

Available Proteins

Throughout the first two-thirds of my missionary life in Nigeria, I was able to buy chicken and beef in the local markets at affordable prices. Most missionaries had taken pressure cookers and cast-iron Dutch ovens to the mission field. Papaya leaves wrapped around hunks of beef did wonders in partially tenderizing it, and all-day cooking in the Dutch oven or extra time in the pressure cooker did the rest.

I learned from a former butcher-turned-missionary that aged beef was far more tender than "fresh" beef, but I also learned that it took greater seasoning to cover the aged odor. Curry and chili powder were both great "cover-uppers."

During my final years in Nigeria, a scrawny chicken, sufficient to satisfy one person, cost about $9. I could buy tinned mackerel and sardines far cheaper, and they became my main "meat." I thoroughly enjoyed them, in both sandwiches and in the hot pepper gravies.

Homeward Bound Again

Humiliating Discrimination

In June of 1967, furlough time had come again and I was flying alone to the U.S., with a stopover in Belgium. The shuttle train took me to the hotel where I was booked for the night. At dinner time I went to the dining room and waited, as the sign directed, to be escorted to a table. Though I was the first person in line, Europeans behind me were led to tables. I, the only American in the room, waited. It happened the second time. After the third group was taken around me to a table, I wanted to sink through the floor from embarrassment. I had no idea why I was being ignored. I knew I was properly dressed, that my hair was combed, and that I didn't look like a lady dressed from a "missionary-barrel." Finally, the main dining room host saw what was going on, ushered me to a table, and took my order. No apology.

The next morning at breakfast, the waiting game—for me—was repeated. White Europeans were being seated. Also black people. Left standing alone, I fought tears of humiliation and finally stopped one waiter and told him I had just a few minutes before needing to board the shuttle train leaving for the airport. I mentioned reporting the treatment I was receiving. This caused him to hurry me to a not-too-clean table. A continental breakfast had been served to the previous guests and a few of the rolls remained in the basket. The waiter brought a clean plate, cutlery, and a napkin. I asked for orange juice and coffee. He brought them. Nothing more.

I finished a quick "breakfast," wiped away uncontrolled tears and dashed to the shuttle train. A black couple with two children was just entering a compartment and I asked permission to join them. They welcomed me warmly. I was back with family—in spite of my white skin. For the first time in my life, I really and truly understood how discrimination can cut one's heart to the core.

Later, in our SIM Home Office, I shared this experience with one of the leaders. He said I was the 17th American to report the humiliating treatment received in that hotel, all because Belgium had a grudge against America at that time. SIM had cancelled all reservations possible.

I was a missionary in the making
wanting to reach out and hug every black person I met and say, "I love you. I know how you have been hurt. I'm so sorry. Please forgive us white people."

My "Permanent" Furlough Home

I arrived in Shady Cove, Oregon to a warm welcome, many hugs, and the feeling that I'd really come home, thanks to my beloved sister Margaret and brother-in-law Joe Bowdoin—and their five precious kids. I claimed them as mine in short order, even though the four oldest had left the nest and were home only occasionally.

It was truly my "furlough haven." The Bowdoin home was located just one mile south of Shady Cove, and I had all that a furloughing missionary could wish for. I called it my "split-level-three-room apartment." Jack and Ivorene Carlton's lovely new camper-trailer became my living room and office (and bedroom for unexpected visitors). Next to it was a tiny building that served as sewing-ironing-miscellaneous room; bedroom was just a few steps away, inside the Bowdoin house. I felt like a queen and lived like one the whole time I was there.

An additional blessing that furlough was Tami, the beautiful German shepherd that belonged to eighteen-year-old Steve, my thoughtful nephew-chauffeur-pal. Tami always welcomed me with her cold, wet tongue. Often, when no one was around, I'd sneak her into the trailer. She was so huge that one of us had to stay put or get trampled on.

Furlough Blessings

My third furlough had come and gone—one overflowing with the Lord's faithfulness and blessing. A beautiful blue Valiant, given to me by Jack and Faye Marie Koken, had taken me over eleven thousand miles to visit family, friends and churches in the U.S. and Canada. Never had I felt more care—more love. It bathed my soul and made me realize in a new way that absence and distance, in themselves, did not, would not, and could not separate missionaries from their co-laborers in the homelands. Only the lack of honest, from-the-heart, communications from missionaries could. I wanted to shout to every missionary on every mission field, *"Write to your supporters. Share your hearts with them. Make it one of your priorities."*

I had been privileged during all of my furloughs to share my missionary experiences in Sunday morning church services where entire families were in attendance, as well as in Sunday School classes and Wednesday night prayer meetings.

Praying women! Those dear servants of the Lord in WMF (Women's Missionary Fellowship) groups in all of my supporting churches were praying for me—and for each missionary the church supported. They continually kept me (us) before the church family by handing out our prayer letters or posting them on bulletin boards.

One such faithful prayer warrior was a dear elderly friend named Carrie. Others in her church told me that as long as she was able to attend Wednesday prayer meetings, Carrie would stand to her feet and say, *"Remember to pray for Mabel."* and folks did. The Lord answered in ways, the telling of which could fill a book. I thanked God for every faithful "Carrie."

Chapter 15
Aug 1967-Oct 1971

Back Again in Nigeria – to Ilorin

SIM – "Sure I'll Move"

*I was a missionary in the making
learning to move out of my comfort zone and into the
"world."*

When asked to move to a new location, we missionaries jokingly repeated our SIM missionary "slogan," *"Sure I'll Move."* I'm quite certain I gulped and asked a dozen questions before saying those words when I was asked to move to the large city of Ilorin.

The move meant enormous changes. It involved a new landscape, a new administration and staff, but also, a wonderfully new open door to share the Lord Jesus Christ outside a mission community and mission schools.

New Landscape

The change from a village setting to a huge city setting was traumatic. I was moving from small bush stations to Ilorin, the capital of the newly formed state of Kwara. It had a population of 2,399,385, and hundreds of VIP were expected to move in to join a large number already there.

The city of Ilorin was home to a large government hospital, huge secondary schools, teacher-training colleges, and shopping opportunities unlike anything seen in outlying villages. Gigantic government generators furnished electricity, sometimes spasmodically, but nevertheless, a real blessing in that they also gave us running water from indoor taps—most of the time. The city had sort-of-paved streets, street lights—off and on, and unimaginable traffic that included motorcycles, cars, taxis, lorries, goats, sheep, chickens, sometimes pigs, and multitudes of human beings on foot.

New People

The special missionary I had come to assist in Ilorin welcomed me with open arms. She was about ten years my senior but did not look it. She had been a School Supervisor in Nigeria for years before being appointed to teach Bible in government secondary schools in Ilorin. She was well acquainted with many of their faculty members—Nigerian, British, and American—as well as with personnel from the various Embassies. She had great rapport with them.

Very soon after I arrived in Ilorin, she had four teas and two dinners to acquaint me with a number of those folks. Missionary M. was totally comfortable with people of high political and social rank, and they with her. It took only a short time for me to learn that she and I were not cut from the same cloth. But she was a wonderful mentor, and I started learning some of her winning hospitality secrets.

For one thing, she made an out-of-this-world chocolate cake. (I never did learn to match it—not even to come close.) But more importantly, she didn't wait for a dustless and perfectly-kept house before inviting folks in for meals—or for coffee and chocolate cake. Folks loved being in her home, and her winsomeness with the many unsaved government personnel reflected the light of Jesus and His love for them.

This dear friend had been given a special little dog, a dachshund named Riro, by a good friend returning to England to be married to her "dream man." I'd not been in Ilorin too long before learning that in a few months, **my** friend would be returning to the States to marry her own "dream man." When I inherited Riro, good friends warned me, *"Be careful, Mabel, you know how Riro's owners end up."*

"Dream men" had evidently run out by the time I gained ownership of Riro, but he became a wonderful pet, friend and watch dog. He gave me a *"Welcome home"* bark each time I returned after school. (I'd left my former pet, Audu, with the missionaries in Omu when I moved to Egbe.)

From Motorbike to Car

When I moved to Ilorin, mission leaders said I could no longer use a motor bike because of the danger. In the early months, I had used taxis to travel to and from school—often with closed eyes and a prayer that I'd arrive in one piece. Before my friend left for the homeland, she sold me her like-new Peugeot. It was easy to drive and totally trustworthy as I drove both defensively and offensively—necessary if one was to get anywhere in Ilorin on time and yet stay alive. No exaggeration.

Out of My Comfort Zone

My first teaching assignment in Ilorin was in a large boys' Government Secondary School, grades 7-14 (included Junior College). The huge faculty, mostly Nigerian with a scattering of British teachers, was entirely non-Christian. I was no longer with a close-knit mission family, with people of like faith and manner of life. A scary thing, but an incredible opportunity was mine.

Islamic Religious Knowledge, with the Koran as the text book, and Christian Religious Knowledge, with the Bible as the text book, were subjects required in every secondary school in Nigeria. Seniors' grades in Bible and the Koran counted just as much on college entrance as science, math, social studies, English, etc. I had a wide-open door to present the claims of Christ to all non-Muslim students.

Teaching in that secondary school had its challenges. Many of the young men were eager to study the Bible, and very few had to be prodded to do the homework assignments. It was a large boarding school, so parent involvement was no issue—for which I was always very grateful. The biggest challenge was to keep up with lesson plans and grading of papers.

It was while teaching there that I had my first and only car accident — a rather humiliating one. After school one late afternoon, several of the Nigeria teachers were standing around in front of school when I started to back up and out of the driveway, waving a friendly "good bye" to them.

Wham! The teachers stared in unbelief as I backed straight and forcefully into a huge tree. I'd forgotten it was there. My face must have registered utter shock because the dear men said over and over, "*Sorry! Sorry! Sorry!*" It was the Nigerian way of showing sympathy.

Mortified, I nodded my head, attempted to smile at the men, changed gears and crept forward, hoping the car would still run. Thankfully it did, and only a very bent-up bumper told friends of my foolish accident. It did teach me to always look behind, forward and to both sides—before moving **any direction.**

Sharing Christ with VIP

Little by little, opportunities came to share Christ with government officials who crossed my path. A reception given by the American Consul was one such opportunity to become acquainted with a lovely American black lady, principal of Queen Elizabeth Secondary School, where I would eventually be teaching. We became close friends, as did others I met there and at other gatherings.

Four single young men and women from England, all teaching in various schools in Ilorin, came into my life.

None of them knew the Lord Jesus, but regardless of that and our age difference (they were in their mid-twenties), we were drawn together. They, Sue, Alice, Martin and Doug, adopted me as their "Mom."

My home became sort of a hangout for them—in spite of three ground rules: No smoking, no drinking, and no sleeping together in my house (they sometimes used the house when I was away for a weekend). Those dear young folks never seemed turned off when I shared my faith with them, and in a real sense, they became my kids. They were definitely non-believers, but caring, protective ones toward me.

A serious water shortage hit the city (wide-spread drought), and I had difficulty getting any water. As long as the shortage lasted, "my kids" found sources of supply and kept my water buckets full—always without my mentioning the need.

At government receptions we attended, they stayed close by, and unashamed, almost proudly, it seemed, told waiters bringing around drinks, *"Our mom would like Orange Squash, please."* The four of them usually hung around, they, drinking their liquor while I sipped my orange drink. The togetherness warmed my heart.

All four left Nigeria at the end of their assignments, but we kept in touch for several years after they reached England. I was grieved that, even in our last communications, they expressed love for me, but none for the Lord Jesus. My only comfort was in remembering that the Seed had been sown and the promise given that it would not return void but would be accomplishing that for which it was sent (Is. 55:11).

She Read the Gospel in Fellow Students

Wonderful FCS retreats (Fellowship of Christian Students) brought together vibrant Christians from the secondary schools and teacher-training colleges in the city.

I loved being with such a mixture of young people, and I even enjoyed the hot, hot foods we ate together.

Timid Shola was one I had met at a retreat. She came to my house one day and shared how deeply she had been touched by what she saw, day after day, in the lives of fellow classmates in her school. As a result, at a Christian Students' Retreat, she had committed her life to the Lord Jesus and stepped from darkness into light, from death into life. Following is the story she told me.

"I watched the small group of Christian girls in the high school. I saw them abused and persecuted, laughed at and ridiculed, yet they refused to fight back. I looked for reactions and saw love and patience in place of hate and revenge. Riots and other student-led troubles disrupted our school. Again I watched that small group of Christians. They took no part, and yet when punishment was meted out, they, the innocent, were the ones who accepted it quietly and peacefully. I kept on watching.

Exam time came and results were out. Many a student wailed and blamed teachers. Not so, the Christians. They had a peace and confidence the rest of us knew nothing about.

Prayer meetings and Bible studies became a forbidden thing in the school, but I saw those Christians meeting secretly in sort of an "underground" fellowship to study the Word together and pray. I began attending and realized those girls had something I wanted. In October, I met their Savior personally, and in meeting Him, I found Someone, not something, who made their lives different. Now I, too, am a follower of the Lord Jesus, but my family does not know Him and I fear to tell them."

In time, Shola shared her faith with her Catholic family and faced ridicule and more, but she was not counted as one dead, as were those who converted from the Muslim faith.

The Holy Spirit used her story to remind me often, in the days that followed, the truth in the following verse:

A Missionary in the Making

"You are writing each day a gospel to men,
Take care that the writing is true.
'Tis the only gospel some men will read—
The gospel according to you."

Some Trust in Chariots—or Dogs

I was a missionary in the making
learning to trust in the Lord Jesus alone.

Riro, the dog I inherited from Marjorie, became a real pal and a super watch dog. He alerted me any time there were steps at the door or around my house. Nigerian friends said that his small size and quick moves were more frightening than those of larger dogs. That was a real comfort and somewhat of a security blanket, as a number of robberies had been reported in the city.

One night I realized that I was depending too much on my little dog for protection.

A friend had asked me to keep a fairly large sum of money overnight for her. Rather than allowing Riro to sleep on his mat under my bed, I put him in the living room to be on double-guard duty, closed the door, and went to bed. Every time Riro barked I sat up and waited to hear foot steps. Time after time I roused and sat up.

Then the truth hit me—from God's Word: *"Some trust in chariots, some in horses* (dogs), *but we will trust in the name of our God"* (Ps. 20:7).

I got up, went into the living room, grabbed Riro and almost shoved him under my bed. I asked the Lord to forgive my lack of faith in Him, my real Protector, climbed back in under the mosquito net and slept peacefully until morning. The friend picked up her money the next day.

Longing for a Spiritual Gift

Some critical situations had arisen and I felt a heavy burden to pray—but my prayers seemed blocked at the ceiling. Among those "situations" was the need for a helper in the yard and around the house. (None of us would have chosen to have house help, but it was a necessity with no washing machines, no lawn mowers, foods needing to be prepared from scratch, etc.)

Seven "boys" (most in early twenties) had come and gone in the previous ten months. Some, because they liked wages but not work, two because of light fingers, one became ill, and three because they had *"just short holidays."*

My faith in praying seemed almost non-existent as the need for help mounted. In desperation I cried out to the Lord for the gift of faith—faith to "remove mountains." Actually, just enough to get a reliable helper. I pleaded with the Lord for it. I cried tears for it as I continued praying. Nothing happened. No reliable lad or lassie knocked on my door asking for a job.

The Lord answered my heart need through a message given by Ken Lloyd. (He, his wife Phyllis, and their children were tremendous blessing to me while they lived in Ilorin. They were one with the nationals, and though many years younger than I, they made **me** also feel one with them.) Ken's message, given in an evening church service, was from Galatians 2:20. One sentence shot out like an arrow into my heart and light burst forth,

"...and the life I now live in the flesh, **I live by the faith of the Son of God.** *"*

The answer was given to me loud and clear: I was to live by HIS faith, and praying was just a part of that living.

Prayers started getting answered. One answer was in the form of a lovely teenage girl named Esther. She became a wonderful, trustworthy helper, a real daughter in the Lord.

Furlough Time Again

"Pst! They are Americans"

It was in the winter of 1971 that Joyce, Thelma, and I had a one-week stopover in England on our way to the U.S. for furlough.

One bitterly cold day while sightseeing in Liverpool, we heard *"Americans"* whispered several times as we passed people on the street. Upon returning to our SIM Guest House, we asked the 18-year-old son of our host and hostess if he could enlighten us as to the reason for the whispers. He was neither timid nor hesitant to do so. In fact, he seemed to enjoy the task.

Five things identified us: We wore **very** nice-looking coats (new ones borrowed from missionaries who had recently returned to Nigeria from furlough) that did not match the rest of our outfits. We wore head scarves tied under our chins—something only factory girls in England wore. Only Americans would wear bobby socks over nylons as we did. Our shoes were definitely not in proper style or color for winter. (Joyce wore white summer sandals, Thelma, almost-acceptable brown brogues, and I, light-colored moccasins.) The last indicator of Americanism was the color of our skin—sallow. Most English girls and ladies had bright, rosy cheeks—not our yellowish, tropical ones.

We wasted no time in getting Joyce to a shoe shop and getting dark dye for my moccasins. Before our next sight-seeing trip, we wrapped scarves only around our necks, left off the bobby socks (and about froze our feet). Skin color, we could not change—no rouge on hand.

A Mixed Message?

I was a missionary in the making
needing to pray hard that the Lord would help me not to
judge others, lest someone point out, not a splinter, but a
huge beam in my own eye.

I had been loaned a lovely like-new car for furlough. Two good brothers in the Lord, both leaders in their churches, felt I needed to have a cruise control in my car. They wanted to purchase and install it for me—which they did. They then asked at what top speed I wanted it to be set. Without thought or hesitation, I answered, *"Whatever the speed limit is."* I was shocked when they tried to convince me to have it set at least five-miles-an-hour higher, because *"everyone drives faster than the speed limit."* Was that one of the gray areas that had crept in— one of which my SIM leader in Nigeria had warned me about finding?

I cringed every time a vehicle, going over the speed limit, passed me and I saw a fish symbol on the back of it. A mixed message? Or was I just suffering a reversed culture shock?

But to be honest, I mentally shook my fist more than once and muttered out loud at/to drivers who tailgated or passed my car and cut in too close. And just as often, the faithful Holy Spirit convicted me with, *"Mabel, bless those who tailgate you; pray for those who pass you on double yellow lines; do good to those who cut in front of you."*

What I really needed and almost purchased was a fish sign to mount on my dashboard right in front of my eyes.

"Use Me," the Fake Vase Shouted

I was a missionary in the making
being reminded anew that only a vessel filled with the Lord
Jesus can offer the life-giving, life-refreshing "Water of
Life" to a thirsty soul. Reminded that outward appearance
can be totally misleading.

What a beautiful blue vase! I saw it on a top shelf in my sister Margaret's storeroom shortly after arriving there for furlough. The vase shouted out, "Choose me!" Which I did and later deeply regretted.

A friend had given me one of the most beautiful bouquets of roses I'd ever received, and I wanted to put it in a special vase. I chose that pretty blue one that had attracted my attention. The roses looked positively lovely in it. I placed the vase on Margaret's tabletop sewing machine and admired the lovely arrangement a number of times before leaving for several hours.

Upon returning, my eyes went immediately to my bouquet of roses. I couldn't believe what I saw—wilted bent-over flowers in a water-soaked vase. A puddle of water under the sewing machine completed the picture.

That beautiful blue vase that had shouted, "*Choose me!*" was not yet a real one. Margaret's son Terell had made it for her at school, but it had not yet gone into a kiln to be fired.

The sight of my almost-dead roses took me back to Nigeria, to a tiny thatched-roof hut in a bush village where I'd gone to visit. The day was hot, humid and dusty, and I was dying of thirst. The gracious little hostess had offered me a drink of water from a clear glass-pitcher covered with a little cloth (like the ones seen in some missionary homes). It was attractive to look at. But....

A large, rather ugly clay pot with a wooden cover stood in a bed of sand in a dark corner on the dirt-floor hut. I knew from experience that the water in that clay vessel was cool and thirst quenching; not so, the lukewarm water in the attractive glass pitcher. I asked my gracious hostess if I could have a drink from the earthen vessel. She disappointedly dipped out a cupful of cool water and handed it to me. It was wonderful, and I was no longer the least bit thirsty. And I was refreshed!

Missionary Barrel & Used Teabags

Outfitting time had come again! It still bothered me, having to let loving friends know of things I needed before returning to the mission field. When asked, I hedged. Until a faithful friend said my pride was robbing other people of blessings. That hurt! But I had needed that love-prompted rebuke. I'd never analyzed my reason for not sharing needs, but I had to conclude that it was indeed pride. Even then, I still found it hard to say, *"I need such and such."*

That should not have been the case because some of the sweetest, dearest experiences I had had during furloughs were times when caring friends from various WMF groups in valley churches gathered to make me lovely dresses, and to bring beautifully embroidered dish towels and pillowcases, etc. I often suggested they not give me such lovely things, and always, always, the answer was, *"We want you to have the prettiest, the best. You need them to cheer you up there on the mission field."*

Loving, sacrificing supporters and friends did that for me every single furlough. No missionary could have been better cared for, felt more loved than I. Never, ever was I outfitted from "the missionary barrel."

On the mission field, we sometimes joked about the "used tea bags" sent to missionaries. None of us ever experienced that. It was true, however, that I liked my tea very weak, and when the price of tea- bags in Nigeria reached 40 cents each, I happily dunked the bag in and out of the boiling water, squeezed it well, dried it out and did the same for at least three days following. It could actually have been used (and enjoyed) another two or three days. Folks agreed that I liked my tea on the weak side.

No Sympathy

On one furlough when I was delayed in New York for medical examinations, doctors asked what my normal diet had been.

I described it as, basically, rice, beans, and the tomato, pepper, onion and oil gravy to which I often added tinned mackerel or sardines, along with wild greens "salad mix" (finely-chopped wild greens covered with water, brought just to a boil, drained, cooled, and fluffed to become the "lettuce") sometimes fried okra with onions, and lots of tropical fruits, along with groundnuts, both raw and roasted. I fully expected real concern and sympathy—and perhaps the reason for some of my medical problems.

After hearing my diet described, the doctors said, "*If all Americans would eat that kind of a diet, we would have a far healthier nation.*"

No sympathy whatsoever. Out the window went my pity party.

Let Me Sink Through the Floor!

One day in 1980, while on a six-month furlough and undergoing tests in Stanford University Teaching Hospital in California, I longed for the floor to open up and swallow me. Never had I been so embarrassed.

Serious loss of muscle strength had brought me back to the U.S. and to that hospital for medical diagnosis. The students and doctors had all read my medical records and knew I was a **single missionary** lady serving in Nigeria.

One team of doctors after another—along with young medical students—filed into my hospital room, checked me over, asked countless questions, took notes, discussed me and departed. After several days of this, I was almost fed up with the questioning and checking and wasn't really "with it" when one doctor asked what had caused the long scar on my tummy.

Without hesitation I blurted out the only thing that came to mind, "*A cesarean section.*" Dead silence followed. The stunned look on several of the doctors' faces told me I'd made a horrible blunder.

I, a single lady missionary had a cesarean section? When I realized what I'd said, I was beyond mortified. As I tried to explain that I had meant to say, "A *large ovarian tumor*," I wanted to vanish through the floor.

Doctors did not find the cause of the deteriorating muscle strength and discharged me a day or two later. I returned to my sister Maxine's home in Lafayette to recover, most of all, from the most embarrassing experience in my life.

Talking with my beloved Stearns family (brother-in-law Bob had gone to be with the Lord), and sharing blunders all of us had made in life, helped me get over the feeling of not wanting to <u>ever</u> see a doctor's face again. I could even laugh over the experience—eventually.

Those weeks with my sister Maxine did wonders in bringing healing of both body and spirit.

"Mabel, You <u>do</u> Have a Gentleman Present"

I was a missionary in the making

learning that independence on the mission field—when no men were around to assist—was one thing; but in the U.S., women needed to be ladies, allowing the male gender to be gentlemen (not an easy lesson to remember every furlough)

In recalling those many good times spent in my brother-in-law's home, I was reminded of a gentle but much-needed rebuke brother Bob gave me one earlier furlough when I had gone to visit them.

He and Maxine were waiting for me in the San Francisco airport. After warm hugs and greetings, we headed down to get my checked luggage. With my usual independence, I had pulled out my check stubs and started toward the carousels. Bob quietly reached out, stopped me, and held out his hand for the stubs, saying he would get my luggage. I almost balked, having taken care of myself all along the way—for many years.

Later, we went to a restaurant and Bob had to literally step ahead of me to open the door—which I was poised to do. The next "interference" came at the table. I was used to serving myself—and others—so I picked up the pitcher of ice water, intending to fill the glasses for all in reach. This time, brother Bob reached out, took the pitcher from my hand and quietly said (message was loud and clear), *"Mabel, you do have a gentleman with you."*

I'd actually been angered by the Women's Lib Movement, feeling it overstepped all bounds that kept women feminine and allowed men to be gentlemen. And there I was "joining them" by my acts of independence.

I blessed that dear man's heart many times thereafter, when men sought to be gentlemen by opening doors for me (car doors as well as others), seating me at a table, relieving me of heavy packages, etc.

A Missionary in the Making

Chapter 17

1972-1982
(Included were three short furloughs)

Back in Ilorin

Queen Elizabeth School

A new school opened its doors to me—Queen Elizabeth Secondary School. Marjorie Cook had left for America and there was no one to take over her classes in the large girls' boarding school. I continued for a time with classes in the upper division of the boys' secondary school, along with the many classes in Queen Elizabeth. It was pure joy teaching approximately 500 students.

Some classes met two times a week, others, three times. For several months, my "classroom" for the largest classes was the auditorium, the stage being my "raised desk"—not the most ideal situation. But I was deeply thankful for the blessed privilege. It was pure joy teaching the Bible without restrictions.

And because the Word, both the written and the Living Word—the Way, the Truth, and the Life, was going forth to many, the enemy of souls was on the rampage, not wanting to lose a single one of his captive students.

He attempted entry through a core of older, non-Protestant students who resented having to be in my Bible classes. Discontentment and rebellion mounted and I agreed with the students that they should not be forced to remain in my class. I was mistaken. A visit to the principal's office resulted in a no-uncertain decision: *All* non-Muslim students must attend Miss Tyrrell's Bible Classes. Finish. Subject closed.

Only the Lord God could solve the sticky situation— and He did by focusing my attention on II Timothy 2:24-25. The words literally jumped out at me.

"The servant of the Lord must not strive; but be gentle unto all men (including rebellious students), apt to teach, patient, in meekness instructing those that oppose themselves; if God peradventure will give them repentance to the acknowledging of the truth."

His ways paid off. In the following weeks the Holy Spirit dealt with that core of rebellious students. He dealt even more deeply in my heart, helping me see that the opposition was not personal—against me. It was against the Lord of Glory.

Not many of the tiny group of rebellious girls surrendered to Christ, but at least they listened to the Word and I again claimed the promise of Isa: 55:11, *"...My Word shall not return void, but shall accomplish that...."*

Brokenness before Fruit Bearing

I was a missionary in the making
learning the need for continual brokenness before the Lord,
the need for transparency in word and in walk—regardless
of the cost.

What's wrong, Lord? Why aren't the students responding? Where am I failing in teaching your Word? The large class of sophomore girls was well-behaved and respectful. But there was no heart response as I taught the series on the Holy Spirit and His power to give us victory over sin—over all and every kind of sin—including unrighteous anger. I was deeply troubled and pleaded with the Lord to show me where I was failing, what I should do differently in teaching the one remaining lesson in the series.

I was running late that morning and asked my teenage helper, to take my dog out for a quick run, something I'd always done myself before driving off to school. Felicia responded with an abrupt *"No."* I was surprised and repeated my request. A second *"No"* shocked me. A third *"No"* (something I'd never before experienced from any of my helpers) angered me to the point of trembling. In a shaking voice I commanded Felicia to take my dog out for a quick run.

The minute my dear helper and the dog were out the door, the Holy Spirit convicted me. Powerfully. Deeply. I fell on my knees and begged the Lord Jesus for forgiveness. Partial peace came. I knew I had to confess my sin to Felicia and ask her to forgive me, but I mentally argued that she was my paid helper and should have been willing to do whatever she was asked to do—especially since I'd asked for nothing unfair. Thankfully, the Holy Spirit did not let me off the hook.

Felicia returned with my dog, confusion and anger written on her face and in her eyes as she threw down the chain leash and marched passed me. When I was able to get her attention and ask her forgiveness, and tell her how sorry I was for my angry words, tears came to her eyes. Together, on our knees we wept before the Lord.

I asked the Lord to fill me anew with His Spirit and headed off to school, feeling peace of heart, but also defeat and shame. The closer I got to Queen Elizabeth School, the more heart-sick I felt. How could I, the teacher, a missionary at that, stand in front of my class and teach God's Word when I had so totally failed Him?

As I entered the classroom, the Lord seemed to say, *"Tell your students of your sin and of My forgiveness, and of My filling you anew with My Spirit."*

I tried to ignore His voice and teach the scheduled lesson. It didn't work. Words stuck in my throat. When I could speak, all I could do was to share with my students my total failure as a Christian. I told them of my confession of sin, both to Jesus and to Felicia, of my Savior's gracious forgiveness, and of His filling me anew with His Spirit. I fully believed I had lost the students' respect, even their attention in the classroom. But an astonishing thing took place. Hands began going up around the room, and girls began standing, confessing: cheating, lying, stealing, impurity, backbiting—on and on and asking for help to get right with the Lord. This went on until the bell rang.

Later, I asked a few of the students—ones who would be honest with me—why it took the teacher's failure and confession of sin to bring many of them into a new relationship with Christ. Their answer stunned me: *I had become one of them—no longer the "perfect" white missionary who stood apart—above them. This freed them from the fear of sharing with me **their** failures, **their** sins, and **their** need of help and guidance.*

It was the beginning of a real work of the Holy Spirit in the school, a work that resulted in students winning fellow students to Christ. Details of it are shared in a later chapter.

A Beloved Friend Dies Suddenly

I was a missionary in the making
learning, in a new way,
to seek God's priorities for the use of my time.

News of Bernice's death shocked me to tears as I lay in our Jos Hospital recovering from a physical breakdown. (Attempting to keep up with schedules in both of the schools had proved too much, and I had ended up in the hospital for almost a month.) Bernice was that beautiful Texas redhead who had so warmly welcomed me that evening when I arrived on my first station. We had spent eight wonderful years together in the teacher-training college before I was transferred to Titcombe College.

Bernice had continued on in WTTC as the beloved Domestic Science teacher. And so much more.

During those first eight years of my missionary life, I had grown to love Bernice deeply, to really admire her. Sometimes I was frustrated by her lateness to the dining room where we other three ladies waited for her, waited to thank the Lord and start eating.

Little did I realize, then, the reason for her late arrivals to the dining-room. Almost always she had been counseling, listening to, and showing deep concern for a student who was in need of spiritual help.

Dr. Jeanette (the same doctor who had helped save my dog, Audu, at Egbe hospital) lovingly, gently shared with me the tragedy that had caused my dear friend's death. The huge steam boiler in the Domestic Science building had exploded just as Bernice was leaving late one afternoon. A large brick had struck her on the back of the head, taking her immediately into the presence of the Lord she so dearly loved and served.

Bernice was to be buried in our SIM cemetery at Miango where the earthly shells of over 50 of our departed missionaries and missionary children had been laid to rest.

Following her death, many of her former students gave testimony to the influence she had had on their lives through the selfless giving of herself (at the risk of offending fellow missionaries). I could never forget those former students' oft-repeated words, *"Miss Matthews was never too busy to listen to me."*

Deadly Lassa Fever Strikes Again

I was a missionary in the making
learning that God's ways are perfect—even when all
human reasoning says, "Not so."

"Oh, to be like Thee, blessed Redeemer,
This is my constant longing and prayer
Gladly I'll forfeit all of life's treasures

Jesus, Thy perfect likeness to wear.

Oh, to be like Thee; Oh, to be like Thee
Blessed Redeemer, pure as Thou art.
Come in Thy sweetness; come in Thy fullness.
Stamp Thine Own Image deep on my heart."

Dr. Jeanette's prayer in song had been shared with us one Sunday morning in our Jos Hospital where I was recovering from that physical breakdown—the same time I learned of my dear friend Bernice's Home going.

A little over a year later, our beloved doctor and friend was able to say to the angels in Heaven, *"I am like my blessed Redeemer, for I see Him as He is."* She was indeed conformed to His image.

The deadly Lassa Fever which had taken our nurse Charlotte a year earlier, and had held Nurse Penny at the point of death for weeks, had again struck in our Jos Hospital.

About three weeks previous to that, Dr. Jeanette had spoken to the mission family and to Christian nationals gathered for prayer. She told them it was time to really trust the Lord and not to panic, reminding them that the deadly virus could not touch a single one of them until it had first passed through the permissive will of a loving Heavenly Father.

That true servant of the Lord, knowing full well the danger, returned with others to continue a ministry of healing to those who had come down with the lethal virus. A ministry to hearts as well as to bodies. (How vivid in memory were the times when Dr. Jeanette had slipped into my hospital room to help lift my eyes to the One who alone could really heal.)

The Sunday after Dr. Jeanette's words to fellow workers, mission leaders radioed mission stations saying that our doctor had contracted the virus. They asked for united prayer. Three days later word came that Dr. Jeanette had gone Home to be with the Christ she loved. We were a heartbroken mission family.

Over and over during that next week, the following words came to mind, *"Greater love hath no man than this; that a man lay down his life for his friends."* (John 15:13)

Contentment – Until...

I was a missionary in the making
needing to learn anew that Jesus was the only source of
true contentment.

Single and content? Yes, very much so—for almost 30 years of my missionary life. The Lord Jesus had been to me all that He promised to be. My life was full and blessed with real contentment in my single state—until "little foxes that spoil the vines" crept in. They did it so subtly.

Fellowship with my dear friend and nearest neighbor Margaret was daily and special. Each evening when I returned from a busy day at school, I'd drop in for a short visit. We'd clue each other in on our day's activities, blessings, and challenges. Being the only single missionary on the station with four married couples, those sharing times were very special to me. Margaret felt the same.

My mornings began about 5:30 with the highlight of the day—time with my Heavenly Father in His Word and in prayer. I'd head off to school by 7:30 and return home about 4:00 p.m. It was an acceptable schedule, a good one actually, one with which I was content and happy—until "the little foxes...."

The first little "fox": I began to notice that the lights in Margaret's house were still off when I drove out in the morning. And off quite early at night. My lights had to stay on fairly late, as I had piles of papers to finish grading, and lessons to prepare for the next day. Almost unconsciously, I began comparing our daily schedules.

Mine, 5:30 am to 10:30 pm, sometimes 11:30 pm; Margaret's: 7:00 am (?) to 9:30 pm. Fair?

The second little "fox": One day I became really aware of something that had always been the case but had never bothered me. As a single missionary, my stove had three burners; Margaret's stove had four (all ladies had four burners in later years). My increasingly subtle reasoning: *I actually have more guests to feed than she does. I have an open-house policy so that missionaries can come in from the bush stations to do their shopping, etc..* (As a single missionary, I could easily offer that hospitality and did so happily.)

The third little "fox": I began really noticing the aroma of roasting meat, freshly baked bread, and other tempting foods when I stopped in for short visits. The thought, *"Margaret has plenty of free time to make special meals,"* crossed my mind.

Late afternoon visits slowly but surely diminished, then ceased. And contentment slipped out and away. Along with joy and peace.

I was still maintaining my early hour with the Lord Jesus, but I was no longer really hearing His voice.

Margaret knocked on my door one evening and I invited her in. More open and honest than I, she poured out her heart, her frustrations, her resentment, her bitterness—her feeling that life was totally unfair.

From her side of the fence, my pasture was green. I had the freedom to get up early each morning and spend time alone with the Lord. When she tried, one or two little lads would be trailing her into the living room crying, *"Mama, Mama...."* At 7:30 each morning, I was free to get in my car and drive off for a day of enjoyable ministry. She was free only to start making breakfast for the four of them, to wash diapers, bake bread, fix a proper dinner, and on and on. Repeated every single day. Week in and week out. Month in and month out. Even the night time was unfair to her. I could stay up as long as I chose; Margaret had to have lights out early at night—according to her husband's timing.

What happened next? Two sinning missionaries, one a very experienced one, and the other, a very young hurting one, were on their knees together, pouring out their hearts to a loving, listening, forgiving Heavenly Father. And asking forgiveness from each other. And realizing in a new way that, "As *for God, His way is perfect...and He makes my way perfect.*" His words, *'Let your manner of living be without covetousness; and be content with such things as ye have, for He hath said, I will never leave thee nor forsake thee* (and) *I have learned in whatsoever state I am, therewith to be content,"* became alive to both of us. The peace that comes with contentment was again ours—in a deep new measure. And so was sweet fellowship each afternoon when I returned from school and dropped in to chat with my dear neighbor Margaret.

Challenged by My Students

At the end of Bible period, Ileautu, Bible Club President, lingered behind the senior class and shared a burden that was heavy on her heart.

A few girls, professing Christians and members of a special witnessing/discipleship group (totally student-run) had spoiled the witness for Christ—before the entire 850 girls, over half of whom were Muslim. Concerned students had spoken to the offending ones, trying to show them the damage their malicious backbiting was doing. They even begged them to resign from the group if they were unwilling to stop their sinning. The offenders resisted.

Ileautu asked if I would speak to the entire group in their Saturday training class. We agreed to pray much before that day.

The Lord heard and answered. By that following Saturday two of the girls had, of their own accord, withdrawn from the group. About forty others met and took a fresh look at the Lord Jesus' requirements for discipleship. A few, finding the cost too great, left. A renewed challenge and vision came to the remaining hearts during the sharing time.

Gentle, soft-spoken Cordelia, a sophomore student, told of her deep joy the previous week in leading two of her classmates to Christ. Others told of similar experiences—and the joy resulting. (The verbal sharing of one's faith was only possible with non-Muslims, but the by-life witness was "heard" by all.)

Never before had I had such a thrilling, humbling experience as I had the two months that followed—the experience of a teacher being led by her high school and college students to pray more, witness more, love more, forgive more, forsake more.

Students had handed me, the teacher, a list of unsaved students I was to pray for until they were led to Christ. They even gave me a second list! It contained names of new believers I was to disciple, *"To meet with at least once a week, more often if possible."*

On more than one occasion after that, I walked in on a student who was busily discipling her assigned family of new believers—at the cost of lunch or supper. (It was a boarding school with no late comers to meals.) And I had thought **my** schedule was too full!

Christmas in Africa

Christmas times were special for us. Celebrating our Savior's birthday was just as precious out there as in the homeland. On one particular Christmas, the burden to reach precious ones still not knowing the Christ of Christmas was heavy on my heart and led me to send the following "sort-of-poem" home to my family and friends.

> *It's Christmas time and thoughts of mine*
> *are rushing home to you;*
> *Thoughts full of love and thankfulness*

for all you've done and do.
For all you are and have been
through the years
As you've shared my burdens and my joys,
my blessings and my tears.

It's Christmas time, and as I write my heart to you
(In very jumbled ways, it's obviously true.)
The thought keeps pressing in—
that you and I have met the Prince of Peace.
But what of ones next door to you at home,
to me out here.
Have they met Him?

It's Christmas time: Christ is our Gift,
our Life, our radiant Light,
But what of ones next door to you at home,
to me out here...
Are they in darkest night?

It's Christmas time; we've Christ the King,
the Christ of Calvary,
And also gifts, and feast, and friends,
and yes, a Christmas tree.
But what of ones next door to you at home,
to me out here?
They, too, have feasts and gifts
and friends and trees.
And bleeding hearts—and fear?

It's Christmas time, and yet do ones next door
to you at home,
To me out here
walk in the night,
While we who know the Christ of joy and peace,
and resurrection life
Withhold the Light?

It's Christmas time, and as I sat
and wrote my heart to you,
In very jumbled ways, 'tis true,
I prayed that you at home, and I, out here
Would love and win these hurting ones
For whom Christ died--and counts, oh, so dear.

Christmas Dinners and "Snow"

Christmas dinners were extra special, even without the traditional turkey dinner and all the American trimmings. Ham, made from "scratch" was one of the treats we had on those and other special occasions.

From "scratch" meant from bristly-hided legs of wild pigs. Hunters somehow found out that I was in the market to take all they would bring to my house. Missionaries from the stations in both Igbaja and Egbe were delighted when "legs" reached them. Buying up all I could pack into my fridge gave me good excuses to visit both stations.

Acquiring real ham took some time and energy, as one had to scrape long and hard to get the wild bristles off the legs and remove the tough skin. The skinned, scrubbed legs of pork were then rubbed down with Prague powder and left to cure. But the cured hams made the time-consuming preparation all worthwhile.

We had no Christmas trees but plenty of "snow"—the white stuff that coated everything outside and in. It was harmattan, the light powdery dust that blew down from the Sahara Desert.

Nigerian "snow" filtered into our houses through regular openings and non-existent cracks—or so it seemed. Five minutes after a "snow fall" and dusting, one could write her name clearly on furniture.

I both loved and dreaded its coming. It brought much cooler weather and eliminated the need for our evaporation cooling system: wet bath towels hung over our mosquito-net bed frames at night, or spread across tummies during the hottest season when nights were too uncomfortable for sleep without that "system." (It reminded me of the burlap-covered food cooler on our back porch when I was a child, and how efficiently it worked.)

Because of the high humidity, mud, rather than snow covered windshields during the harmattan season. Windshield wipers moaned as they dragged over the glass, hardly keeping up with the soggy gray stuff that accumulated thick and fast. Believe it or not, I found it somewhat exciting to be out driving during those days. Reminded me of Oregon snows I sorely missed. The same was somewhat true during rainy seasons when I drove through slippery mud— Nigerian "black ice."

Odd things brought unexpected pleasures—ones that were hard for folks at home to even imagine.

Steaks: Rat, Snake & Monkey

A terrific noise in my neighbor's back yard drew everyone's attention. Two boys were shouting and wildly beating some object with long boards. The shouting was ear-splitting. When missionary Marilyn and I saw the reason, there was complete understanding. A feast was in the making.

A two-foot-long bush rat soon lay dead. Marilyn's houseboy and his friend built a fire, burned off the animal's fur, and took the rat to the sink for a thorough scrubbing.

Later the meat was carefully divided into three parts, and Marilyn was presented with her share. She praised and thanked the boys for their unselfish thoughtfulness and told them she wanted them to have all of it. They were delighted to re-divide the meat because their diet seldom consisted of such luxury.

Only three times did I have difficulty eating meat or chicken—all considered very special—graciously and unselfishly offered to me.

On the first occasion, a really beautiful-to-behold white snake steak was put on my plate; on the second occasion, a hunk of monkey meat; on the third, a crispy, deep-fried chicken head with eyes intact (a favored part of the chicken). All three times I took a small bite or nibble, struggled to swallow without "losing it," and thanked my unselfish, caring host or hostess. And left as promptly as courtesy would allow.

I loved those dear people who wanted to share their very best with the "white mother." Those totally unselfish people often put missionaries to shame with their giving—most often out of their extreme poverty.

Feeling Overlooked

I was a missionary in the making
learning that sharing with others a hurt, a
misunderstanding, or just a loneliness, brought deeper,
sweeter fellowship—to all concerned.

As the only single missionary on our SIM compound in Ilorin, there were times I felt both lonely and overlooked—totally my fault. The four married couples with children were all really friendly and caring toward me, and not one of them had an inkling of my left-out feeling.

The lonely "overlooked" times came when the families prepared picnic suppers and drove out of the city to eat on some safe, rocky plateau—away from hiding snakes.

The couples all knew that I needed to spend each late afternoon and evening grading papers and preparing for the next day's lessons. I'd not kept it a secret. The secret I had kept was that I just wanted to be invited to go with them. It was silly, knowing that I'd have to refuse. But I still longed for the invitation.

If only I had been more open and had shared my feelings of being overlooked on those picnic excursions! When I did—much later—the married folks were stunned and said something like, *"If we'd only known! We'd have loved having you with us."* And I knew they meant every word of it. They proved it again and again.

Unique Wedding Cake Decorations

A wedding was soon to take place, and Esther, my faithful house girl had asked if I would make her wedding cake—a four-tier one. Making the cake, though a challenge, was not a problem, with borrowed cake pans from a missionary who had brought some in her outfit.

The big challenge came in finding things to make it really look like a wedding cake. The "things" turned out to be large hollow plastic hair curlers, 6-inch meat skewers, pipe cleaners, and heavy cardboard to go between the layers. We pushed the meat skewers through the tightly stuffed hair curlers (covered with aluminum foil) to make the pedestals that would separate the layers. After frosting the whole thing, we put on the top ornament—an arch made from pipe cleaners, two sugar-like bells suspended from the cluster of lily-of-the-valley flowers, and a poof of nylon netting (all items brought in "outfits" from the homeland). We thought the finished product was rather lovely—like a real wedding cake.

The biggest challenge was ahead—transporting the rather-weakly-constructed "masterpiece" over 50 bush-road miles to the village where Esther was to be married. Dorothy drove while I balanced the 4-tier cake on a pillow on my lap. It was a good thing we had forced the skewers through each layer, each pillar, and then through tough cardboard. The cake and we arrived a bit shaken, but in good shape, overall.

However, I'd made one serious mistake in "building" it: forgetting to leave a slit in the cardboard under the bottom of the second layer so the bride and groom could cut a piece to feed each other. But they managed to dig out sufficient cake to do the trick.

An incident, totally unrelated to **that** wedding, is worth sharing here.

Early in my time in Nigeria—before some of our students understood our new-to-them ways at weddings—a concerned student asked a surprising question (we had attended a missionary wedding together). *"Why did the bride and groom (missionaries) bite each other at the end of the wedding?"* Explaining the difference between biting and kissing posed a bit of a problem, but I **think** my explanation of one of our ways of showing affection to special people eased the student's mind. At least I hoped so.

Praying "Elijahs"

I was a missionary in the making
continually thanking the Lord for my faithful prayer
partners in the homeland whose prayers availed much.

It was only as I regularly shared specific requests with prayer warriors at home (and answers to their prayers) that miracles kept happening. The following letter, sent home to my supporters and prayer partners back in 1975 is an example:

My dear faithful "Elijahs,"

Elijah of the Bible prayed that it wouldn't rain. Not a drop fell for three years and six months. Then he prayed for rain and it poured down. God heard that man's prayer of faith and He answered. And He's hearing yours and He's answering.

Because you prayed, this missionary's foot is greatly improved and tormenting back and head pains are less and less frequent.

Because you prayed, mountain-high barriers of bitter family opposition are gone. Esther (for whom I made the wedding cake) and Sam are free to begin a Christ-centered home. This influential couple, a college lecturer and a government stenographer, prayed and waited—and suffered—not wanting to marry until parents gave willing consent (though Sam was a committed Christian, he was from a different dialect area in Yorubaland). Their witness of patient trust in the Lord spoke to many young people's hearts.

Because you prayed, Victoria has deep, sweet triumph in the Lord Jesus—in spite of a heart deeply torn as she broke off her engagement to a young man. Other young people, seeing her courage and trust in the Lord for her future, will likewise bravely choose the lonely pathway of purity—lonely—except for the Savior who walks beside them all the way.

Because you prayed, I've been able to complete, with joy and patience (most of the time), the heaviest school term ever (and one of the most fruitful) of Bible teaching. His strength alone, the direct result of your praying, has made this possible.

Because you prayed, many of our youth are discerning between Biblical practices and those of Satan, and many are daring to live for Christ in this difficult, challenging time.

One of them is Ajadi. Serious illness came, forcing him to leave college and go home. His upset family, feeling his recovery under professional medical care was too slow, sought help from the medicine man. Knowing its connection with Satan, Ajade refused it and was driven out.

A bit later he staggered to my door, too ill to stand. Christian brothers took him to the hospital. Day by day, for nine long weeks, the Lord provided money for food, medicine, etc. What a witness Ajade left in that place! The love of Christ was felt through him as he ministered to others in the ward—even though terribly ill himself. Muslim patients watched, accepted that ministry of love, wondered, and finally, just before Ajade was discharged, asked him to tell them about his Jesus.

Languages Galore

Can you imagine a country having about 470 different ethnic groups and languages? Nigeria does! However, there are three major ones: the Hausas, located in the Northern States, the Yorubas, mostly in the South Western States, and the Ibos, located in the South Eastern States.

My people were Yoruba, with a difficult tonal language I was never able to really master.

I was so very thankful that English (British English, mind you) was the trade language throughout the country, and the only one allowed to be spoken in the secondary schools and in dormitories—for the sake of unity.

Only on Sundays and when visiting in the villages, did I hear and attempt to use the little Yoruba I had learned in my first term on the mission field. Foolish pride—starting away back then—kept me from practicing it. I had allowed a senior student's ridicule of my laughable attempts at speaking Yoruba stop me from even trying. If only I had laughed with her and kept practicing!

One day I awakened to the reason for that dear girl's ridicule. She was in my English class and had failed the subject—**my** language. She somehow reasoned that her only recourse was to fail me in speaking her Yoruba language.

I was heartsick when I realized, too late, how foolish pride had blinded me to the need of that hurting student whose "ridicule" was probably a cry for help. She was failing in all of her subjects.

That experience stayed with me over the years and helped me, numerous times, to overlook cutting, critical words that seemed to erupt from students with deep, hidden hurts—students lashing out at the teacher in a cry for help.

My Former Student Now My Doctor

I was a missionary in the making
learning the blessedness of a two-sided ministry.

I needed to have a GI examination—a rather personal thing. The British doctor arranged for me to have it in the University Hospital in Ilorin. That was fine—until I learned that one of my former student librarians from Titcombe College would do the examining. He had graduated from junior college, gone overseas for his medical training, and had returned, a skilled internist. I dreaded for the appointment day to arrive.

Arrive it did. I checked in at the front desk of the hospital and was taken to the doctor's private office. He, and several other former Titcombe students—now doctors there in the hospital—had planned a surprise get-together for their "Mama Tyrrell." I had to fight back tears as they greeted me. We sat together reminiscing. The young men talked of our times in T.C. and expressed appreciation for my influence in their lives. We drank ice-cold Orange Squash, ate cookies, and had a wonderfully heart-warming and informal time together. My "boys" couldn't have been sweeter. After about 30 minutes, they all left for their various offices and appointments.

The time had come for the dreaded examination. A Nigerian nurse led me to the small room to undress and put on the hospital gown, then on to the examination room. The specialist there was no longer "one of my students;" he was a very professional, impersonal doctor, and my fears dissolved. The non-embarrassing examination was completed, and I could have hugged my boy-student turned my-skilled-doctor.

Ministering to Me

Bill Crouch's words of praise regarding Nigerian brothers and sisters in Christ, words spoken over twenty years earlier to a brand new, almost-disillusioned missionary, had been proven true over and over and over again to that very missionary. Me.

But it was during some of my last years in Nigeria, when I was alone in the city of Ilorin, that Bill's words became living reality in my life.

Qualified, dedicated Nigerians had taken over the responsibilities of all of the other SIM missionaries in Ilorin and had moved into their houses on the compound. I was surrounded by wonderfully caring and precious black brothers and sisters who adopted me as their own—to watch over, to take care of, to meet my every need. Which they did willingly and lovingly day in and day out.

Grace and Isaac Jimba lived next door where my good friend Margaret had lived. Fellowship with them was beyond precious. It was the same with Stephen Akangbe and family—and with others.

Living alone among them had broken down barriers which normally existed if one lived among missionaries who were always quick to help during times of sickness and other need. My forced dependence upon my black family opened the floodgates for poured-out blessings. And they came—immeasurably—as I shared my spiritual needs, my failures and victories, as well as physical needs with them.

I would not have traded those precious months for anything in the world. They were filled with Christ-centered relationships, deep sweet fellowship, binding-together love, and rare oneness of spirit—memories of which I will treasure for life.

Rescued by God's Black "Angel"

Peter was just that—God's black angel—sent to me in a time of real need. Esther, my spiritual daughter, had married her Sam, and I needed a helper I could trust.

Peter became that helper—more than a helper, actually; he became a real son in the Lord. He was around 19 years of age, had grown up in the SIM orphanage at Oro Agor (the one I visited soon after arriving in Nigeria), and was a plumber's apprentice by day and my helper by night. He lived in my garage room (self-contained—after a fashion), and was as faithful as the day was long.

He was my teacher of patience and humility. If I spoke sharply to him about something he had done—or not done—and started to apologize for my unkind tone, Peter would invariably say, *"Please, Mummy, it is my fault. I forgot."* or *"I was careless. It was not your fault."* His humble spirit and gentle words invariably left me feeling two feet high—and wanting to be a better example, a more loving "mom" to the dear lad whose self-image was too low to measure.

Peter had lost all of his front teeth during a fall when just a child in the orphanage, and it had deeply affected his self-confidence—even in relationships. Ilorin had a dentist by the time Peter joined my household and he was able to have a totally new look—with beautifully white teeth showing each time he smiled. It gave him a much-needed boost on the road to self-respect.

Over the months, Peter became more than just my "right hand." He became my confidant. And courageous rescuer. I could never forget the night he risked his life for me.

The Biafran Civil War (1966-1970) was raging in Nigeria and the city of Ilorin was under a strict curfew, dusk to dawn. Fear was rampant in the country. Thousands of Ibos, living in the north, were attempting to flee south to their homes to escape the horrific massacres going on; likewise, the Hausas were attempting to escape to their homeland in the north. (It felt as if our "middle belt" was in the center of it all.)

We missionaries had been warned to heed the curfews. Thugs, hired by the opposing sides, were often high on dope and could not distinguish between black and white people.

On one particular afternoon I had driven to the compound of a sister mission a short distance away and had not watched the time, allowing darkness to creep in. Peter, deeply concerned for his "Mummy," sneaked out of his room and walked over the back roads to rescue me. (He knew where I had gone.) All had been warned that violators of the curfew would be shot on sight. Peter, being black, was far more at risk than I, a white person, would have been. But that didn't matter to him.

That dear, dear lad led me by hand through the darkness over back roads to our compound, then in through his garage room to safety. With pounding heart, I thanked the Lord that no soldier had spotted my courageous black angel, and I thanked Him over and over again for that dear lad who had become a real son in the Lord.

Final Nigerian Assignment

Igbaja Experiences

I was still a missionary in the making
learning and growing as I witnessed young adults leaving
all to follow Christ, and others, enduring a terrifying
disease, yet triumphant in Jesus.

A new location, a new SIM family, and a new
challenge faced me in 1982—the move to the SIM
compound near the small village of Igbaja. I was
scheduled to teach in the Igbaja Secondary School located
on the hill.

Plans changed. The greater need was for a registrar in
the ECWA Theological Seminary, located on the adjoining
campus just down the hill.

When told of the change, all I could again say was,
"*Sure I'll move*"—right into another impossible-without-
the-Lord situation. A registrar's responsibilities were
totally foreign to me. And upon first glimpse, frightening.

Processing and screening of student applications, and
scheduling interviews and entrance exams for many of
those out-of-state as well as in-state applicants were some
of my duties. Mistakes on my part could have jeopardized
students' entire futures—and tragically hindered the Lord's
work. Many an SOS for prayer again flew across the
ocean to prayer warriors in the homelands. And they did

not fail to pray! God, in His infinite power and mercy, answered those prayers and gave the wisdom needed to meet each daily demand in the registrar's office.

Loving, concerned students prayed, too. They were all university age or older, about half were married, most were men, and all were there in the Seminary and Bible College because they had chosen to leave all and follow Christ.

What an encouragement many of them were to me— often when I needed it most. We had many opportunities to chat since academic warning slips, etc. went out from my desk. This opened the door to sharing burdens—both theirs and mine. Many of the students were keenly aware of the deadline pressures in the office and of my need of encouragement. Every morning I received many a warm smile and a cheerful greeting from students passing my office window on their way to a 7:30 class. Some wrote wee notes of encouragement—or from-the-heart advice. Example: *"Dear Mom, please cooperate with the Lord and rest more. I'm concerned and am praying for you. Your son, Paul."* Others sometimes left an egg (about 40 cents each), or a yam, or some oranges. Many dropped in at my house for a short early evening visit. You would have loved them as I did.

Did those young men and women really sacrifice to learn God's Word? A few examples give the answer.

The "Three Musketeers," so called after they enrolled in the seminary, had been drawn together. They became special sons in the Lord to me. They were single and in their mid-twenties. Paul, called to become a pastor, left a lucrative, ego-building T.V. career. Richard, a prince of a young man and well educated, was gloriously saved when serving time in a prison. Lukeman came from a solid Muslim background and paid a huge price when he chose to follow the Lord Jesus rather than a lucrative career.

Peter, Mercy, and their small son had come from a distant country. They were an educated, cultured couple. With baby on the back and 3-yr belongings on heads, they trekked for the first two days (a new experience). Testing came fast and often after their arrival at the seminary— Satan's efforts to discourage. But the enemy failed!

He tested many others through similar ways: illness, lack of funds, even some infant deaths. But the Lord held them steady and faithful.

Terrifying Disease—yet Radiant Joy

When possible, we visited churches other than the large one in Igbaja. One Sunday morning I entered a small church in another village, one especially for those with leprosy. I expected to see sadness, discouragement, discontent, self pity, even some anger. But most of all, hopelessness. I was astounded at what I saw.

The perfectly-formed, beautiful little girl smiled at us from the bench just ahead. Her young mother and she didn't seem to belong in the small group of tragically deformed and crippled people among whom we sat. An older woman reached out to take the restless little girl— reached out with fingerless hands. I cringed. True, their disease was arrested, and they were non-infectious, but still.... A few minutes after that, the mother of the toddler reached to take back the still restless little one, and I understood the reason those two, mother and daughter were in that little group. The lovely young mother had only knobs for fingers, and a toeless, incomplete right foot. Her face, still young, beautiful, and alive, had somehow been spared from the ravages of leprosy. Her baby girl was still beautiful and whole.

I looked around at the people in that small congregation and saw LOVE, JOY, and PEACE. I even felt it as they stood (some, painfully and awkwardly) to welcome me. A bit later, they followed the fingerless song-leader in joyfully singing hymns of praise. The lump in my throat kept me silent.

The pastor, an educated man, but one who belonged to their company of suffering (his deformed hands revealed it), opened the Word to that small group of believers who listened with hearts wide open.

After the service I visited outside some of their homes for a few minutes, homes that consisted of just a room or two, empty of almost everything the world required for comfort.

Again I felt something beautiful and rare. Contentment. Contentment in the faces of a people bereft of physical wholeness, of society's acceptance, of even basic essentials. I witnessed a rejoicing people. A people actually radiating the love of the Lord Jesus. And a peace that most of the world knows nothing about.

I left that little group counting my blessings as never before.

Two of a Kind

We were definitely "two of a kind"—the Fiat car and I. Somewhere along the way, my faithful Peugeot had given up and I had purchased a **new** car that needed one repair job after another. Both of us chugged along with make-do parts since new ones were not available in our section of the country.

The Fiat sounded like a teenager's hot rod with its improvised Peugeot muffler, while I sounded like I'd lost my two front teeth when my lower denture broke in half and was held together with scotch tape—until the tape became wet and the denture again parted. I was able to teach through a 45-minute class before that happened, and I always had scotch tape at hand—to do another repair job—in private.

Later, metal solder (for mending, I didn't know what kind of items) did a more "permanent" temporary job. It wasn't too long before I was able to get truly professional help with denture mending.

Again, about my car: It was a necessity, even for short distances, because my foot and knee were less "roadworthy" than the vehicle. Daily I thanked the Lord that both of us were able to keep going.

"Please Don't Send Me Home"

I was a missionary still in the making
learning that the God of all compassion was still working
in love—even though, at the time, my heart questioned it.

"Please, let me stay here. I know I can recover if I just stay in bed and rest." But the answer was, *"No, you need medical help which we cannot give you here on the station."*

High fever, loss of appetite, and extreme weakness had again hit me and nothing seemed to bring healing. I was unable to get up from a chair—or stand—without help. Muscle strength was gone. Missionaries took me to Egbe to be under doctors' care. Several weeks there, with no improvement, meant a flight to Jos for tests and the opportunity to "let rest restore." Restoration did not come.

My world crashed when caring, wise doctors consulted and agreed that I needed to go on a medical retirement— needed to go home to America. Not for a furlough but to stay!

"Good Bye"

I was flown back to Igbaja to say final "good byes" and to pack up—which I was unable to do. Concerned and loyal friends, Donna Welch and Joyce Flint, did the sorting, selling, giving away, and packing for me. I rested in the warmth of their care and love—and hard work. And in the same loving warmth of the SIM family and Nigerian Christians I had grown to love so deeply. But I felt torn apart at the prospect of having to leave them.

Five to six-foot-high grass covered the tiny airstrip at Igbaja. It was on that tiny strip of land that the mission plane, scheduled to take me to Lagos, was to land. The airstrip wasn't even visible! Until several hours later.

Students in the secondary school left their classes, and with two-foot-long banding-iron grass cutters (cloth wrapped around the ends for hand holds), mowed down and removed the grass, clearing the airstrip. I broke down and cried when I heard what those willing-hearted students had done.

With loving boosts, I boarded our tiny mission plane and whispered, "*Good bye*," to Yorubaland where I had spent 34 wonderful years.

I confess that my final flight from Nigeria to LaGuardia Airport was not filled with the sacrifice of praise to my Heavenly Father. Rather, I questioned and argued with Him. *I wasn't ready to retire. I did not want to be put on the shelf. Couldn't I have regained health if I'd stayed on longer in Nigeria? Had I really been so ill that I needed to be sent home?*

It wasn't until later that I was told that beloved missionary friends who put me on the plane heading out of Nigeria wondered if I'd even reach the U.S. alive. I was glad I didn't know their "wonderings" on that final flight to America, under the care of a compassionate missionary sister flying home for furlough.

The weeks spent in our Mission Headquarters in New Jersey were healing, comforting, and encouraging, as SIM USA Director, Larry Fehl, assured me of yet a future. (I had become well acquainted with Shirley and Larry when they were at Igbaja Seminary (Larry was principal) while I was still in Ilorin. They moved to Jos when Larry became a dedicated Field Director in Nigeria. I had learned to deeply respect his leadership and to trust his counsel.)

The infection and fever gradually disappeared, and I was able to leave the wheelchair, and though still very weak, board the plane for the U.S. West Coast. An unknown future lay ahead, and yet I was assured in my heart that the Lord wasn't finished with me yet.

I was still a missionary in the making
being prepared for a new mission field.

Chapter 19

July, 1985

Home Mission Fields

Shady Cove—My Home—Until...

I was a missionary still in the making
learning that our Lord's mission fields are even in nursing
homes.

"There is no place like home." I found this to be so true once I arrived at the Bowdoins' place in Shady Cove, Oregon. They insisted it was to be my home for as long as I wanted. What a comfort that was! I needed time to recuperate and to seek the Lord and His will for my future.

Larry Fehl had suggested I check out SIM's two retirement villages in the West, one in Sequim, Washington, and the other in Carlsbad, California.

With two sisters and one brother and all of their families in the southern state, that seemed the ideal place to settle. But a visit to our Carlsbad Retirement Village helped me to realize that I did not want to become a city person, much as I enjoyed my time there with the SIM missionaries and admired the beauty of the place.

A few weeks later, a retired missionary friend and I visited the SIM's much smaller, yet lovely retirement home in Sequim, Washington. Our two days spent there, and much prayer, convinced me that my new home was to be in Sequim, the area known as the "banana belt."

To the "Banana Belt"

I returned to Shady Cove and prepared to move to Washington. In the summer of 1986, Joe and Margaret Bowdoin helped load a U-Haul and off we went on Interstate 5. I had acquired a new-to-me car, and it was loaded to the top with household goods. Margaret, with their car equally loaded, followed, with Joe and the packed-to-the-ceiling U-haul bringing up the rear as we drove up the gorgeous Hood Canal highway and into the small town of Sequim.

We spent that first night on mattresses spread on the floor. Margaret and Joe stayed several days to get me settled in. They were a blessing beyond measure, and it hurt to see them leave. I knew no one in Sequim other than Elda whom I had met on that first visit.

The Ben Owens, SIMers who had served in east Africa until Elda's broken health brought them home, had built the six lovely, two-bedroom duplexes and had given them to SIM for a retirement center. I was the first SIM retiree to have the blessing of moving into one of them. What a wonderful place to settle! The landscape was gorgeous and the climate was unbelievably tropical—without the humidity.

The friendship and fellowship with Elda Owens (Ben had gone on to be with the Lord), who lived in duplex #1, were very special gifts from the Lord to this newly "retired" missionary. Very soon I felt at home and ready to discover my new mission field.

Every Sunday afternoon, Elda played the piano in two nursing homes for the worship services. I had the joy of going with her and getting to know some of the precious folks there. I even began visiting during the week.

A Different Kind of Mission Field

"Lord, could this be Your place of ministry for me? I need to be needed, to be able to share Your love with

others." The answer came just a few days later when I was visiting in the nursing home.

The activity director approached me and asked, "*Mabel, would you be willing to become our volunteer manicurist? We really need one, and you seem to have an interest in our residents.*"

I explained to her that I knew absolutely nothing about doing manicures—that I'd never even had a professional one. She chuckled and then described what my job would be.

I would enter the residents' rooms carrying a shoe box with rose-covered wrapping paper—one familiar to the residents—so I'd not be a stranger. In the box would be emery boards, polish remover, and several colors of nail polish. My most important job would be to give the much-needed personal touch—something vital to the residents (some had no families ever visit them). Most often I'd just be a caring friend, patting a hand or arm, offering a listening ear—doing those things most needed.

I was thrilled with the idea and told the activity director I would be there the next day for the orientation hour. I went home on cloud nine, thanking the Lord for the exciting new mission field.

And thus began four years of a precious ministry to the often-forgotten ones, the hurting ones in nursing homes. The most alone ones I've ever seen—alone in spite of people all around them in beds or wheelchairs.

Among other instructions the activity director had given me in the orientation hour was the following: "*Remember that a resident (never called a "patient") may hear and understand everything that is said in his/her presence, even if there is absolutely no evidence of it.*"

I had kept that in mind when visiting in the various rooms, but I hadn't realized the full import of her words until one day my eyes were opened.

One precious little elderly woman had always lain motionless curled up in a fetal position. She seemed oblivious of anything going on. In past visits in the room, I had only patted her shoulder and moved to the next resident. One day I felt led to sit down beside her, pat her arm and quietly share some Scripture. I started slowly quoting Psalm 23. When I reached: *"He maketh me to lie down in green pastures"* I saw a tear squeeze out of the corner of one eye, and her lips began forming the words, *"He restoreth my soul."* On through the rest of the Psalm we went, I, quoting the words aloud, and she, forming them with her lips. It almost broke my heart, thinking of the many times I could have been ministering God's word to this precious, lonely little sister in the Lord.

About midway through my nursing home ministry, the activity director asked me, really urged me, to come into the nursing home at any time, day or night, when a resident might be nearing death. I'd had freedom to share my faith with interested ones right from the beginning, but this was a wide-open door to share Christ with the ones in deepest need. How I thanked the Lord for it, and I took every opportunity to enter that "open door."

Where Now, Lord?

After four very happy years of volunteering in nursing homes, I knew a change was needed. *"Enough bending over beds and wheel chairs,"* my aching back shouted.

I was not ready to retire to a rocking chair. No way! I hoped—I almost knew—the Lord wasn't finished with me yet. So I prayed, prayed, and prayed some more, seeking His will, hoping for another mission field.

Final Mission Field

New Hope Christian Schools

Do you remember the little lad named Terell and the "tough-love" I had witnessed just before leaving for the mission field the first time? God had begun, away back then, the making of missionary Terell who, years later, was to head up New Hope Christian Schools, a non-denominational Christian school holding a clear Biblical worldview.

I knew it would be a blessing to serve in a school that considered missions as one of its priorities. Five, from the very first teaching staff, left NHCS to serve on foreign mission fields, and others followed suit over the years.

Many of New Hope's graduates have gone into full-time ministries for the Lord, both here in the homeland and on foreign fields, while others are God's "light" and "salt" on college campuses, in the business world, and in their homes.

It was to my nephew Terell, principal of the school, I wrote, asking if I could join the staff as a volunteer—doing whatever was needed.

In October, 1990, I said "good bye" to many of the folks in Sequim who had become dear friends and headed home to Oregon—to Grants Pass—to space #10 in the NHCS mobile home court.

I was really back to stay in the Rogue River Valley where I'd spent most of my life before going to Nigeria. Back near family, beloved friends, and faithful supporting churches. Back to minister in my "Jerusalem." And yet still on a mission field—New Hope Christian Schools—with children of all ages, preschool through grade twelve.

I felt "at home" in the school. My brother John had helped build it, brother-in-law Joe was a founding Board member, nieces and nephews had graduated from it, and others were current students. I'd visited the school on most furloughs to share Nigerian experiences and challenge students to be missionaries in the making.

As elementary school vice principal for ten years, I had many opportunities to talk with parents desiring to enroll their children in NHCS, among them, some parents who had not yet met Christ personally. A mission field? Yes!

In the following years, I continued on as a member of the administrative team and assisted in the business office and wherever else needed. I was richly blessed with the responsibility of keeping in close touch with our school supporters and prayer partners who were the real life-line in the school.

A special joy was the privilege of fellowshipping with the many senior retiree volunteers who came from all over the U.S. to help at New Hope.

Each time a couple from SOWER's (Servants on Wheels Always Ready) or MMAP'ers (Mobile Missionary Assistance Program) rolled into the RV Park across from our mobile homes, I rushed out to greet them with warm hugs and, "Welcome, fellow missionaries!"

The retired builders, contractors, engineers, secretaries, teachers, dentists, administrators, etc., (many having gone through heart bypass surgery and back surgeries) had come to volunteer a month's work in the school. The men would jump right in to meet any need on the to-do list: construction, masonry, electrical work, plumbing, ditch digging, installing playground equipment and windows, painting, renovations—whatever needed to be done.

I had the blessing of coordinating the ladies' work in offices, classrooms, painting, sewing, picture mounting, etc. They lifted many a heavy burden, those willing-hearted ladies!

What a gift these volunteers have been over the yeas, not just to NHCS, but to many non-profit Christian organizations. A wide-open door for yet more retired folks to become missionaries in the truest sense!

A Missionary in the Making

Chapter 21

A Missionary Still in the Making

Continuing to Grow

At the time of this writing, I am still serving in NHCS and continuing to grow in the Lord Jesus.

One of my greatest joys is the opportunity to challenge students in classrooms and chapels to live for Christ and to be missionaries, **today,** in their own "Jerusalems," and— someday, if the Lord calls them, to carry the **Good News** beyond the shores of America.

I am "Aunt Mabel" to students and staff alike and receive many a heart-warming hug from both. Though many years older than all on the NHCS staff, never do they make me feel old—just "older." Nor do they treat me with "kid gloves," something I deeply appreciate. Fellowship with all is heartwarming.

In addition, I have a wonderful surrounding "family" here in the school court. Remember my black "angel" in Nigeria named Peter? Two white "angels," Lloyd and Dreda, live just two mobiles away. They keep close watch to see that I'm ok and they help in a multitude of ways. How blessed I am!

In Matt. 19:27, The Apostle Peter asked the Lord Jesus what one would get in return for following Him. In case he is listening from up Yonder:

*"Peter, you get "a hundredfold" of all you have left behind. **I've proved it.** I have a world-wide family in SIM with its 16,000 active missionaries from 37 nations serving*

in over 40 countries (plus a large number of retirees), a large New Hope Christian School family, and a large family of other brothers and sisters elsewhere. Yes, Peter, you can't out-give the Lord of Glory!"

My Challenge to You

As you read *The Making of a Missionary*, did you observe that the **mission field is**

"Here" in "Jerusulem"—one's town and neighborhood,
"There" in "Samaria"—one's school, college, work place,
"Out yonder"—in Nigeria & in "the uttermost parts of the world?"

Did you see that a **missionary is**

One who **tells forth** the Good News that Christ died for all,
One who **lives out** the Good News—the only Gospel some will "read?"

Did you notice that **missionaries are**

Nigerian students in secondary schools & colleges,
Young Nigerian adults: doctors, teachers, etc.,
Older Nigerian adults: church leaders, laymen,
And "Sent ones" from America, England and other lands?

Did you witness **the cost** of following Christ?

The loss of loved ones (both babies and adults)
The loss of position and power
The loss of family (especially Muslim)
The loss of financial security

Above all, did you see and feel the **"hundredfold" blessings** that one gains when he leaves all to follow the Lord Jesus?

I challenge you, teenager, young adult, baby boomer, retiree to answer God's call given to Isaiah (Is. 6:8).
"Whom shall I send, and who will go for us?"

I warn you, it may cost all you have—even your life in the days ahead, but regardless, will you answer with Isaiah,
"Here am I; send me, Lord"?

A Missionary in the Making

Conclusion

Was God's Way Perfect? Was He Trustworthy?

Did the Lord keep His promise to me, His missionary, that He would <u>be all</u> that I needed, and would <u>provide all</u> that I needed? Yes! One hundred times over!

He was closer to me than any earthly father, husband or children could ever have been. He gave me a family of beautiful mixed color, spiritual children, comfortable homes "beyond number," and immeasurable eternal riches.

And so much more!

- ❖ He gave me, a person with normal physical desires, contentment in my single state, and He kept me pure.
- ❖ He gave a peace that passed all understanding.
- ❖ He gave strength for each day, enabling me to *"mount up with wings as (an) eagle, to run and not be weary, to walk and not faint."*
- ❖ He gave me fun times. Happy times. Countless joy-filled times.
- ❖ He gave hope when things seemed hopeless.
- ❖ He gave victories when the enemy sought to bring discouragement through much illness and physical weakness.
- ❖ He gently encouraged, comforted and went before me every step of the way.

And through it all, He patiently and lovingly continued reshaping and refining—all needed (and still needed)—to make me an "earthen vessel" He could and can use.

I pray that all of you who journeyed with me through *A Missionary in the Making* will have seen that

"As for God, His way <u>is</u> perfect."

A Missionary in the Making

Appendage

Several friends have asked that I share some of the culture shocks I experienced over the course of my missionary life—for the sake of new missionaries going to foreign fields. I doubt that similar ones would be true today—in some cases—but for the sake of those who requested this, I am letting you in on a few of them.

I was well prepared to face real differences in African culture and was able to adjust fairly easily to different living conditions, foods, language, etc., in Nigeria. What I wasn't prepared for were the "cultural differences" between white people: American vs. English (British) that I experienced in the fifties and sixties.

Our **speaking** differed in word usage and pronunciations. Our **spellings** differed. Our **math** differed. Our **style of eating** differed (the use of knife and fork). Even the **time and way we served some foods** differed. Our **social customs** differed. Here are a few descriptions of those differences that "shocked."

❖ **Spoken & written language**: It took many months for my students to even understand my American speech and spelling. Their experience had been "British."

❖ **Food:** British inspectors occasionally ate with us when at WTTC on inspection tours. I learned early on NOT to serve them pancakes, syrup, and eggs at the same meal, or a carrot and pineapple jello either before or with the main course. Twice, when I had done so, my horded jello, <u>untouched</u>, slowly but surely did a "melt" down. We Americans loved mixing sweets with savory. Not so, many from the Continent.

❖ **Method of eating**: The use of knife and fork differed drastically. So much so, that a British acquaintance asked if we Americans kept picking up our knives to cut meat, then putting them down while we chewed just "for show." I was both amused and shocked at her question.

❖ **Social customs**: We Americans loved our potluck get-togethers, unannounced visitors popping in for a meal, even our doing the same with others. We thought nothing of doing so—until one Christmas. Thelma and I were alone on the station. Alone and lonely. We knew that our English neighbor, two miles away, was also alone. Her husband was out on trek. Thelma and I decided to take our baked chicken and trimmings in to share with P. who had just recently come from England. We sat at her table, with our food on one end near us, with her food on the other end near her. Unknowingly, we had committed a huge social blunder and totally embarrassed our dear new friend. Before the meal ended, we had eaten some of her food, and she, some of ours. We returned to our station two wiser, more thoughtful people, realizing that, in England one did NOT take food to another's home uninvited, unannounced. <u>Months</u> later, we three could laugh over our differences and appreciate them.

❖ **Greetings:** On one of my return trips to the field, I was detained in our SIM Home Office in New York (my foot needed a longer time to heal after surgery). During my waiting time there, I was asked to befriend a new missionary candidate, a lovely young lady from the Orient, who was having difficulty adjusting to the American culture—an adjustment needed before she went on to the mission field to live with missionaries. I found, in short order, that our way of greeting and showing friendship was completely offensive to Lin (not her real name). One morning she seemed to be even more withdrawn than usual so I began asking her questions—just to show her I was interested in her welfare, that I really cared. My questions went something like: *"How are you this morning, Lin?"* *"Did you have a good night of sleep?" Do you have any special plans for today?"* Lin responded with absolute fury, accusing me of asking personal questions that were **none of my business.** I was stunned and I attempted to explain that I was only trying to be a friend. After that "exchange" between us, I walked on egg shells whenever we were together. I hurt deeply for Lin who was having such a difficult time adjusting to American people and culture. Lessons I learned from that experience helped me other times when I attempted to become a friend to one from another culture.

❖ **American "shockers":** Astounding as it may seem to some people, I faced big "culture shocks" in my own homeland.

1. **Buying new clothes:** Trying to buy dresses with totally different size labels was one of the first shockers. Even two dresses marked identical sizes wouldn't fit the same lady! I was so very thankful for "twice new" shops, with dress sizes I recognized and often, like-new designer dresses, in styles I felt comfortable wearing, and ones that fit my budget.

2. **Buying groceries:** An even bigger shock came when I tried to buy groceries and faced dozens of different brands of each item. I hadn't a clue which one to select.

3. **Seeing food wasted:** One of the most hurting shocks came when I saw "tons" of good food being thrown out—in homes, schools, restaurants, and grocery stores. I thought of the millions of children starving around the world and just wanted to sit down and cry.

4. **Witnessing a "new morality":** A disillusioning shock hit me as I observed the rapidly disappearing line—in Christian circles—

between black and white areas of morality: new terminology replacing old, what was once unacceptable for people of faith to listen to, watch, read, discuss, and laugh over, now seemingly acceptable.

Yes, I must confess that the greatest shocks came when I tried to readjust to life in America.